Cover: Shiva, Parvati and Ganesha enthroned on Mount Kailas with Nandi the bull. Chromolithograph by R. Varma.
Credit: Wellcome Collection (https://wellcomecollection.org/works/dmv-7fu7a). Attribution 4.0 International (CC BY 4.0) (https://creativecommons.org/licenses/by/4.0/)

Back cover: Hanuman, the monkey god, holds a mace in his right hand and a Himalayan mountain, with the herb sanjeevani, with his left. Gouache painting by an Indian painter.
Credit: Wellcome Collection (https://wellcomecollection.org/works/dmv-7fu7a). Attribution 4.0 International (CC BY 4.0) (https://creativecommons.org/licenses/by/4.0/)

Translation: Decody – House of Translation

Copyright © 2021 Swami Manuel
All rights reserved.
ISBN: 9798749864724

YOUR CELLS EMBARK ON A JOURNEY

DISCOVER YOUR GIFTS, BREAK FREE FROM ADDICTIONS AND EGO, HEAL YOURSELF AND ENTER A NEW STAGE IN YOUR LIFE

A Journey to the Temples of Krishna, Saraswati, Hanuman, Kali and Ganesha

Swami Manuel

DEDICATION

*Even if you are hundreds and thousands of
kilometers away, you are always nearby.*

"no distance"

CONTENTS

INTRODUCTION..11

LESSON 1..21

  The Beings Inside You

LESSON 2..29

  Two Ways of Communicating With Your Cells

LESSON 3..41

  Self-Healing and Improving Your Health:
  The Temple of Krishna

LESSON 4..61

  Developing Your Gifts and Missions.
  Self-Knowledge:
  The Temple of Saraswati

LESSON 5..89

  Working On Your Addictions:
  The Temple of Hanuman

LESSON 6...111

  Overcoming Fears Caused by Ego:
  The Temple of Kali

LESSON 7...135

  The New Stage:
  The Temple of Ganesha

EPILOGUE..155

ACKNOWLEDGEMENTS

To each and every one of the mistakes I have made and the difficult situations I have been through.

Without them I would not have made it here.

Introduction

With this book I want to introduce you to a course unlike any of my other courses. I am not going to talk – at least, not much – about chakras, auras, haunted houses, positive and negative energies, protections, etc. Today I want to invite you on a great journey to your innermost self that is bound to surprise you. On this journey I will reveal the existence of the different kinds of intelligence contained within yourself: that of your cells and their memories (lower beings) and that of your Higher Being. When I say "lower beings", I do not mean this in a derogatory sense; on the contrary, I am referring to the simple beings with a very basic form of intelligence that make up our bodies, the wisdom of single cells or groups of cells. "Higher Being" is what I am going to call our pure connected being, the spiritual intelligence that is contained within each and every one of us and that must control the baser intelligence of our lower beings.

INTRODUCTION

Cells have a simple, almost binary intelligence. They are constantly deciding how to relate to one another, and are often, as I will later explain, influenced by external agents.

Have you ever wondered what is stopping you from reaching your goals? From the classic examples of working out, studying or learning a language, to small daily activities. Do you know what is behind those moments when you think "I'm too tired…", "I don't feel like it…", "I'll do it next week…", "On Monday, for sure…"? Let me tell you: it is the cellular memory of your lower beings influencing and even controlling your actions.

Have you ever asked yourself why some people develop their gifts to sublime extents? Why does an artist create such wonders on canvas? Why does a violinist draw such melodies from a violin? Why are some people so successful in business? Why does a writer put so many wonders to paper? Why do some people have inner peace? Why are some people so full of energy? What's more, why are some people always happy and healthy?

A human being is not a single intelligence. In every human are two main intelligences: the intelligence of cells or groups of cells, which we will refer to as lower beings; and the intelligence associated with the positive power of your mind, your soul and the universe, which we will call Higher Being, and which must be in control of your thoughts and actions.

A Higher Being is one that acts with purity, nobility and coherence. I do not believe the Higher Being to be the soul, though it is related to it, of course. One might even say that the Higher Being is the representation of the soul in this life.

This course aims to help you master your lower beings to help your Higher Being reach the goals it sets out to accomplish.

As I Ching philosophy expert Carol K. Anthony rightly states, with their simple intelligence, our cells receive, for instance, a stimulus indicating that their reserves are low, and we receive in turn a direct, unequivocal message: "I am hungry" or "I am tired." This message is accompanied by the urgency of having to solve the problem. If we set out to make a meal, this sense of urgency will relax as the Higher Being accepts the demands of the lower being. So far this might seem a normal, irreproachable reaction. But, to pursue the example of food, if our lower beings take control and are not subdued, they can continuously send messages asking for food, for sweet or even for smoking, alcohol or lying down. They can make you think you don't want to work out, and even encourage addictions to certain people or situations. They can make you feel afraid…

On the other hand, by controlling them we can encourage, stop or eliminate altogether this unwillingness to do certain things, as well as the urge to do other potentially harmful things. The results are truly surprising.

Your cells' simple intelligence must never hold sway over your higher intelligence; that would be taking a step back in your evolution. We were bestowed with higher intelligence (Higher Being) to evolve, and to evolve is to be in control your life, not to have it be controlled by the cravings born from memories planted in your lower intelligence (lower being).

Your cells have their own memory, and it is this memory that influences your decisions and sends messages to your Higher Being. This memory has an acquired component from the moment we are born, through the experiences we live and the external stimuli we receive. If from the moment we are born we are bombarded with media messages portraying false standards of happiness, that information will reach our cells and their decision-making processes will be influenced by them.

Can a pianist have such extreme control over his fingers without having his lower beings on a tight leash? Absolutely not. Throughout his training, his lower beings sent him countless messages announcing pain, tiredness, the inability to go on… But the pianist's Higher Being subdued them in such a way that it achieved its goals.

Can you imagine what we can accomplish by learning to control our being? Can you imagine being able to convince, overcome or even eradicate those things that hinder your ability to advance and stop you from reaching your goals?

If we go back to the example of our lower being's pressing demands for food, it appears that if we obey these demands and set out to cook, the feeling of hunger lessens somewhat. The Higher Being sends the message to act upon the requests of the lower beings and that simple action is enough to placate the feeling of hunger. This proves that the Higher Being (whose nature is vastly more complex and powerful than that of the simple lower beings) has the power to manage and quell the trivial demands of the lower beings.

The next step is to learn how to send messages to your lower beings without giving in to their demands, when these are toxic for your personal growth and health. This is the goal of the course: to master your lower nature in order to gain inner peace and success in the broadest sense of the word.

If our lower beings are spoiled because we regularly give in to their demands and they are steeped in materialism, falsehood, ego, fear, etc., then your gifts (yes, we all have many) and your projects will continually be sabotaged.

This course is going to be mostly practical. The exercises will consist in guided meditations to help you learn to control your lower beings and incorporate this habit into your daily life. This process will guide you to a new personality. Through these meditations you will learn to tell a coherent demand from an unreasonable one. That way, you will take the reins of your body and mind.

With this course, you will not only gain control over your lower beings. As you practice the exercises and the meditations, you will also cleanse yourself by getting rid of all those things that have been engrained in you, leaving a pristine empty space that moving forward only you will be in charge of decorating.

The course consists of seven classes or chapters that include methods or guided meditations to learn to control your innermost self. Meditations are deep sources of self-knowledge, information and development. With these five guided meditations you will travel to your inner temples. Your inner powers are represented by the deities of these temples. In them you will find strength, answers and I am certain that even an affinity hard to put into words.

Perhaps that is one of the cornerstones of Hinduism: the affinity of its deities with our inner powers. These meditations will become your tools for wielding power over yourself. Eventually, you will not need guidance and make the meditations your own. Although we are going to work on specific issues, the exercises can be applied to all things in life that stop you from advancing. They will help you with everything you need to work on. It will surprise you just how many fields they can be used for. For instance, these tools can help you control tiredness, laziness, rage, anxiety, disorientation and even weight loss. The possibilities are endless. What you decide to use them for is in your hands.

As you can see, I advocate the power of meditation. It is one of the most efficient tools for self-knowledge and self-improvement. My experience meditating in temples has sometimes been so powerful that I owe them much with regards to my progress. To meditate, one must rid the mind of obstacles that prevent us from connecting with our soul. In other words: to meditate, we must reconnect with our childhood, with that part of life when fantasy was a tool for connecting with the impossible. It is more than just fantasizing; it is connecting with the deepest parts of ourselves. I would love it if you don't follow my instructions to the letter and add the variations that best suit you when meditating and practicing these exercises.

Right now, you might be feeling the effects of your lower beings as they attempt to persuade you to stop reading. They might be sending you messages like:

- I am not ready for this.
- I don't have the time.
- I'm finding it hard to concentrate.
- It will be a waste of money.
- These courses are all the same.
- What will my family think if they see me doing this course?
- I am too tired.
- It is too late to learn these things.
- I feel fine the way I am.
- This is not for me.

Do any of these voices sound familiar?

By the way, I recommend you always have a bottle of water at hand. You will understand why during the second lesson.

I will teach you, through exercises, one of my simplest and most important healing methods. Water, ever present, is a source of life. I also recommend you have paper and pencils nearby so you can write down your goals before practicing each meditation.

Regarding the formats and wording of this book, I have included some additional comments in italics, as if they were footnotes. I also occasionally write in the feminine form. I believe some grammatical norms are hundreds of years behind the reality of today's society.

LESSON 1

The Beings Inside You

We are an infinitely complex combination of inner physical and energetic connections (microcosm) and complex connections to the world and the universe at large (macrocosm). You are a single abstract point. The connection between your microcosm and the macrocosm is your Higher Being. It is hard to define what the Higher Being is. We could perhaps define it loosely as the intelligence that should be free from external interferences and that connects the two cosmos and manages the avatars of life. We could say that the soul lies behind your Higher Being, we might even be able to say that the Higher Being is an avatar of the soul in this existence.

Your Higher Being has clear functions: to remain in harmony with the soul by controlling our physical and social interactions and by developing our potential; and, on the other hand, to connect with the universal.

The Higher Being might reside in the mind and to reach its goals it must have maximum control over your being.

Within you live billions of lower beings. Simple beings with limited intelligence and scarce functions. Every cell in your body is a lower being. Lower beings are the ones in charge of managing specific aspects of your physical and emotional mechanisms. They group together to form tissues, and the tissues form organs that allow the human body to function.

In this course, we are going to focus our attention on this functioning, and especially on the relationship between your Higher Being and your lower beings.

We are independent existences, and yet we depend on the forces that balance our environment. Everything we see, feel, eat, drink, love, laugh at, read, touch, desire... all these things have an impact on the Higher Being and on the lower beings. Managing these influences, be they positive or not, has to be in the hands of your Higher Being, as it is the one endowed with greater intelligence. The Higher Being is able to decide what to accept and what to reject. The parameters will depend on the gifts or missions life has in store for us.

The problem is that the lower beings do not solely perform their basic yet highly important tasks. They are also influenced by the world and, putting their tasks

LESSON 1 – THE BEINGS INSIDE YOU

aside, they sometimes try to decide what is the right thing to do. Unfortunately, they do not have the capacity to make these decisions as they do not have a global vision, only a narrow one. When they receive inappropriate stimuli, they can come together to send messages to the Higher Being warning about non-existent needs or unrealistic dangers. Lower beings are easily manipulated. It is up to the strength of the Higher Being to make sure they stick to their tasks.

I do not mean to say that the messages of the lower beings are always negative. They are mostly necessary for the proper functioning of the organism and the being in general. Messages like "I am thirsty", "It hurts", "I am sad", "I am happy" broadcasted by the lower intelligence of your cells are indeed necessary messages that the Higher Being will then go on to manage. But, for instance, if when watching TV commercials we are suddenly shown a refreshing drink, the lower beings send a manipulated message begging you to quench your thirst with said drink, even when you are not really thirsty. If the Higher Being repeatedly gives in to the demands of the lower beings, it runs the risk of losing its control over them and will then give in to just about any external stimuli. It is okay to occasionally indulge the lower beings, as long as we do not lose control over them.

LESSON 1 – THE BEINGS INSIDE YOU

The lower beings are not only at the mercy of TV commercials, but also of all sorts of interactions with other people, society at large and any positive or negative energies one may be exposed to.

I believe we are born with a correct relationship between our Higher Being and our lower beings. The intoxication begins when we are a few months old. This is not a new phenomenon; it has always been this way.

I am going to make a bold assertion, which I believe to be mostly true. Many bad decisions we make in life are the result of our lower beings taking control. Taken to the extreme, many crimes are a consequence of this. As well as countless blocks, diseases, addictions, fears and lives spent without discovering the wonderful natural gifts we all have. The control of the lower beings over the Higher Being is an anti-natural intoxication of the soul caused by external agents and false stimuli. The lower being falls for the promises of false happiness it receives from the manipulative agents of society.

There are different degrees to which the lower beings can be intoxicated, with their corresponding consequences for the Higher Being. To find out to what degree one is intoxicated one has to undergo a process of self-knowledge and deep self-criticism. There is an exercise I often recommend to gain this awareness and measure the degree to which your lower beings are intoxicated. It consists in giving up certain things for a period of time. This exercise is more than just a way to measure the control you have over your being. It is also a practical exercise for "reeducating" your lower beings. It is by practicing exercises like this that we become aware of their existence. For instance, when we try to quit TV or social networks for 24 hours, the struggle and temptation we feel comes from the lower beings. That is when you identify them! That's right: they are the ones who talk to you, the ones who tell you to go online, that the exercise is pointless and so on. If you give up sweets or fast, the same thing happens: they bring about the sense of anxiety that dynamites your efforts. So many examples, right?

Of course, not every cell in your body is out to boycott you, only certain groups of cells that can be spread out in different parts of your body.

You might be asking yourself, how can these cells be intoxicated by external agents if they are not exposed to them, if they don't have eyes or ears. Their eyes are your eyes, their ears are your ears, their pleasure is your pleasure, your temptations are their temptations, and the same thing goes for your joys and your disappointments. Thought it may feel as if I am talking about two separate entities, that is not the case at all. You are a single entity: you are a cell, a group of cells and your Higher Being.

When you are conflicted, you experience a civil war, not a battle against a third party.

It is well known that humans have outstanding potential and strength. In extreme situations, we are able to draw strength from unknown sources when moments ago we didn't have any. These extreme situations are like a smack in the face for your lower beings and your entire being; they are necessary to achieve some goal of vital importance. This just constitutes further proof that power, control, lies in the hands of the Higher Being.

Awareness of the existence of these two blocks usually rises from our problems. Hardships make us realize something is wrong, and the cause often lies in having let the lower beings take control. Let's imagine someone who is unemployed and lives with his parents. Instead of, for instance, learning a language or signing up to a course, he doesn't do anything out of pure laziness. The lower beings, who are always loathe to change, send the primal message of having to save energy and not make any big efforts. That person does not have his lower beings under control and is subject to their will. As long as he remains where he is, nothing will happen; but the moment he decides or is made to go, he realizes he has a problem, he understands that something inside him was holding him back. The problem of having to survive without his parents' protection makes this person face a crisis. This might make him wake up and get his lower beings under control. That is only one example, but it can be applied to any kind of change. Another example: a broken couple. To go on without making any changes in the relationship can be a result of the messages of fear the lower beings are sending to the Higher Being. Fear of change, fear of living alone, fear of being without company, etc. When it is inevitable, the problem can lead to our becoming aware of the manipulative effect of the lower beings that are boycotting our will to make changes. Disorientation, anxiety, depression, sadness, moodiness, disease, addiction, negative isolation, bad decision-making, self-destructive behavior... Many are the examples of the ways in which the lower beings can block us when they are in control. Problems can often lead to great progress.

This way, the external enemy (another of the lower being's tricks) disappears. Blaming others, society, the fact that you are misunderstood, etc. may feel out of place because we have ceded control to these negative stimuli. Of course the terrible structure of society is at the root of many of our problems. Society and its rules have always been the cause of trouble and they always will be. But now the battle is going to be waged in your innermost self, where these manipulative energies should never have arrived and prospered in the first place. And that is going to be the nature of this course: pure inner work geared toward self-knowledge and healing.

Talking to your cells is not a fantasy. From now on, this course is going to focus on talking to them and trying to rid them of the influences that manipulate them and make them ill. To establish communication with them, we must first strengthen our union with them. We are fully aware of our mind and our thoughts, but we are not usually aware of the simple thoughts of our cells or groups of cells. We are mostly distant, almost to the point of detachment, from their thoughts.

LESSON 2

Two Ways of Communicating With Your Cells

In this second lesson we are going to practice communicating with our cells or groups of cells by using two practical methods: communicating through the direct method of meditative introspection and through charging water with vibrations to target a specific issue. These are "all-purpose" exercises you will be able to use to work on any physical or spiritual matter. I think their efficiency will surprise you. The second exercise, charging water with vibrations, should become a daily or almost daily habit. When you read it, I hope to properly convey its importance.

The Introspective Method for Communicating With Your Cells: The Parachutist's Perspective

Your Higher Being has great unknown powers over your body. It is from this Higher Being that we are going to contact each and every cell or group of cells. Thought is only one of the abodes of your Higher Being and we are going to use it. I would like you to locate a cell or group of cells within your body. The main goal of this lesson is not to treat a disease (though we will, of course, touch upon that in later lessons), but to learn to locate them and master a method for treating them. Let us establish contact, for instance, with the cells of your heart. I usually use certain parts of the body as communication paths, such as the nervous, digestive, respiratory, circulatory and lymphatic systems. But I am often not even aware of these paths: you simply find yourself using them. Everyone can choose the system they feel most comfortable with. These systems are the roads along which we are going to travel to our destination, a small cellular "town" or cellular unit. What is fascinating about these excursions is that, from the outset, we establish a connection with the cells that conform the path, as we will now see. Although this book is called Your Cells Embark On a Journey, we will first have to travel to the cells in question, to meet them and gain control over the access paths. Later, they will take centerstage.

LESSON 2 – TWO WAYS OF COMMUNICATING WITH YOUR CELLS

Let the journey begin. I recommend closing your eyes to focus completely on your inner self. Starting from your mind (it tends to be the starting point), we are going to gather the essence of your Higher Being. We can imagine this essence like a sphere of light in which we have concentrate our higher energy. Create, mold, knead that sphere of light. Use your hands if you wish. Take your time, think about light and what it means for life, for the plant and animal kingdoms, and hold it tenderly between your hands. Once your have created this sphere, slowly, the journey begins. Let's move it and make it travel through our body. On the way to the heart, you will make occasional unplanned stops to gather more light. A powerful point at the start of the journey is the Ajna, the brow chakra. You can feel it a bit above the space between your eyes or even right between them. It feels like this point, the eyes and their cells, add light to the travelling sphere. We continue the journey down to our sense of smell and when we breathe in we add light to the sphere. You are breathing in light. We go down to the throat and by breathing through the mouth we continue to brighten the light. Once we are at the height of the center of the chest, at the heart chakra, source of universal love, breathing throughout, we wrap our sphere in layers of light filled with love. At this point the roads become narrower and more meandering until we reach the heart. Its beat accompanies us. The sphere of light leaves in its wake a trail of life, of gifts from our Higher Being. Inside the heart, within its tissue, we draw closer and see millions of moving points. We see them from a great height, as if looking down at them from an airplane. We lower the healing light and descend with it, we parachute down from an imaginary plane, slowly dropping and choosing the spot where we are going to land and flood with sun-essence. We can now make out the individual cells that conform this cellular mass. To me they look like spheres huddled closely together, looking, happy and intrigued, towards this light that is approaching. I focus on a smaller group, one of twenty or fewer, and start to direct the Higher Being's message of light impregnated with love towards them. I imagine rain falling in slow motion, like snowflakes. I focus on one cell in particular in harmony with those around it, which in turn harmonize with those around them. I place a large sphere of light and life upon them, I cover them in light and slowly each and every one of these cells drink it in and make it their own. They receive the message of unity with the Higher Being and they feel healed, strong and able to continue in this way. The entire sphere of light dissolves into them. The memories that distracted them fade and are replaced with positive memories. There is no return journey as this is a journey into your innermost self.

Well done.

I encourage you to practice this exercise to treat any kind of physical or emotional discomfort. If it is physical, its location tends to be clear. If it is emotional, search inside yourself for the place where the affected emotion lies. Believe in yourself, do not harbor doubt. Once located, bathe that place in light.

Perseverance is always necessary when dealing with energies. You might have had the notion of single miraculous actions planted in your mind. I do think this can happen, great progress can be accomplished in a single session, but like all things in life, it takes practice. Through perseverance you can reach your goals.

The Method for Communicating With Your Cells Through Water Vibrations

I have spent many years talking about the amazing effects that water charged with intent can have on our physical and spiritual body. In almost every single one of my attendance-based courses, we practice charging water with vibrations. We do not usually give much importance, from an energetic perspective, to goods we have in plentiful amounts such as light and water. Some higher being might be looking down at us in desperation upon realizing that we are surrounded by these energetic treasures but don't give them the credit they deserve, beyond their purely physical uses.

We are now going to practice carrying energy to a specific point through water we will charge with vibrations. As with the last method, you can use this exercise on any part of your body that needs healing, be it physical, energetical or emotional. You can ever charge water so that it will reach your entire being, and not just a specific point. Let us work, for example, on non-natural tiredness. We are going to reach out to the cells that cause this sense of exhaustion without a clear cause. Our job is going to consist in transferring powerful energies through water that will mainly be charged by your Higher Being through its connection with the universal.

Hold between your hands a glass or metallic bottle of water. The water inside it must be as pure as possible. If your running water at home is not too polluted, it will do just fine. If not, I recommend you use bottled water.

I usually imagine tiredness without an apparent cause as a place without much light in which cells start to doze off. Our goal is to take light to these cells to reawaken them. But how do we know where to find these cells? They are hard to locate as they can be scattered throughout the body, though I believe the brain, the heart and the muscular system are all likely targets. This tiredness might also be the physical or emotional manifestation of a problem, which makes its source even harder to

LESSON 2 – TWO WAYS OF COMMUNICATING WITH YOUR CELLS

pinpoint. That is why this water method we will use to send our vibrations is so effective.

Your Higher Being is the complex intelligence that must control your lower beings. It is connected with the physical, with the earth and with the universal. This connection will help us impregnate the water you are holding with millions of spheres of light. These millions upon millions of spheres of light will be in charge of enriching the tired cells and, on top of that, they will also bring light to those parts in need of energy. One of the many functions of your Higher Being is taking care of your lower beings, your cells. Let us deliberately put that function into practice.

While holding the bottle, and focusing on your Higher Being, you are going to travel to the universal. You are going to go looking for light to contain it within billions of particles or photons of light. To that end, your Higher Being is going to raise its energies towards the sun. Close your eyes, if you wish, and feel your crown chakra (located at the top of your head) open and broadcast energies towards the universe. Imagine these energies being attracted by our source of light: the sun. As they rise, they form a cone or funnel with the narrow end on your crown chakra. The funnel opens up to the sun to capture as much light-essence as possible. You are creating a mechanism for attracting light-essence. This funnel gathers large amounts of light and makes it flow into a concentrated part of yourself. With every breath, picture yourself breathing in these photons or quantums of light. Billions of them are softly falling into your Higher Being. Billions of tiny spheres of pure concentrated light are softly and continuously falling onto your crown chakra. From that point, from that point of entry to the universal, from your Higher Being, the river of spheres of light runs down your brow, your throat, to the center of your chest and from there to your arms and hands and into the bottle of water, which will absorb it all. The billions of microspheres of light slowly penetrate the water and charge it, as if it were a battery of infinite power. Look at the water if you wish.

You are connected to the sun, reaping its fruits and delivering them to the water. Along the course of that inner river, your body's cells are also enriched. Your Higher Being can help you feel this course. You might feel a tickling sensation in certain places; they are vibrational reactions to the flux of light.

When you see fit, and thanking the source of light for its fruits, you slowly shut off that channel and focus on yourself. It is time to give instructions to this treasure you hold between your hands. You are going to ask the billions of water molecules, the billions of light-filled hydrogen and oxygen atoms they are made up of, to

LESSON 2 – TWO WAYS OF COMMUNICATING WITH YOUR CELLS

pour into the tired cells that are making your feel tired. Tell these molecules made of atoms filled with universal light that they are going to become a part of your being. Tell them they are going to become a part of you, of the 75% of your body that is made up of body. Ask them to reach the furthest corners of your organism and especially to bathe those tired cells in light, and let that water be the water that regenerates those cells.

You can also tell them about yourself, your life, your loved ones and what you will do with the energy to make them all better. Talk to it – you will only be talking to yourself –, talk to that water that is going to become a part of you. And tell it that you want that water to capture any negative elements it encounters and wash it out your organism. The water is going to bathe your cells one by one, leaving only purity behind, expelling the residues of this cleansing.

When you see fit, once again proffering thanks, open the bottle and drink mindfully, fully aware of what you are achieving. Drink while reminding yourself that you are drinking light and that from your mouth this light will travel through your digestive system, into your blood and throughout your body.

Drink and be grateful.

Clearly, I think you are quite aware of the many ways you can use this method of cellular treatment. Your lower beings receive the light and increase their positive connection with your Higher Being, which is now back in control.

Well done.

Although this course is aimed at yourself, at your being, it might occur to you that you could enrich water for other people. That, of course, is perfectly possible. It is a beautiful exercise, to charge water with positive vibrations in order to help somebody who needs an energy push. In these cases, it is best to use empathy, to not judge nor impose ideas. You need to respect the other person. The added message must mainly be one of love, never one of imposition or of willing a certain action. It might be best if you do this after completing the present course, because, as you will soon see, we are going to try to eliminate many ideas and memories that are currently lodged inside us.

Visualizing light to charge the water is only one of many ways you are surely going to discover. You can think about nature, the earth, plants, rain, clouds, the sky... Anything that is natural in origin and connected to the universal.

Let me tell you an interesting story. Years ago, I met a group of travelers in a hostel. Most of them were traveling alone or in pairs. Usually, the conversations that arise in this type of situations fall within the parameters of formality, though we did start talking about energies. For some unknown reason, one of those people started to laugh uncontrollably. It was lovely to see her laughing. I took a bottle of water from a nearby table and placed it between her hands, unable to explain to her why. Her laughter increased as she was holding the water bottle. After a few minutes, it started to wind down. It goes without saying that her laughter had spread to all of us. She looked surprised when she noticed she was holding a bottle of water and asked what it was doing there. I told her to give some water to the person sitting next to her, and she did. The other person drank and instantly burst out laughing, making us all laugh again. Without realizing, she had charged the water with happiness and, by drinking it, the other person had received its effects. Not everybody agreed with this assessment, but as they drank, they all successively started to laugh.

With these first two lessons we have discovered the existence of the inner intelligences (lower beings) contained within our cells or groups of cells, and that of the higher intelligence (Higher Being), your being's main intelligence, the one that must control the rest. We have explained how external influences affect and plant memories in our cells and the need to free them from these memories derived from the superficial aspects of life. We have practiced two exercises to connect with and heal cells or groups of cells and, as a result, we have meditated. We have also learned to channel our energy, with all the advantages for our physical and spiritual health that this entails. And lastly, we have opened the door to treating other people with our energy work.

LESSON 3

Self-Healing and Improving Your Health: The Temple of Krishna

From an energetic perspective, physical discomforts appear when a part of your body is not receiving the continuous flow of energy it needs. The physical area, that specific point (or points), is not sufficiently nourished in order to function properly. These tend to be weak points that are found all throughout our organism, but there is no reason why they should appear prematurely. This happens when some sort of energy block hinders energy from flowing properly to these points. A faulty flow can be due to several causes, from an emotional block, bad habits or a hard energetic environment to a lack of harmony between the soul and the actions you perform.

LESSON 3 – SELF-HEALING AND IMPROVING YOUR HEALTH

During this lesson we are going to connect with the affected areas to destroy the negativity that is afflicting them and thus help them return to their normal state. I am aware of how difficult it is to work with energies when we are suffering from physical pain, but I hope that when you feel the positive effects the pain will not only vanish but also help you become more aware of your own power. With the two exercises we practiced in the last chapter I hope to have piqued your curiosity and helped you obtain results that will encourage you to continue this great inner work with renewed strength. Through those exercises we practiced two forms of healing that I have no doubt will already be a part of your regular exercises. But let's take things a step further.

In the first lesson I told you about the lower intelligence of cells or groups of cells. As I have said before, when I say "lower" I do not mean it in a derogatory sense, but in the sense that this intelligence is limited and basic. A cell has very little decision-making power. According to a study carried out by the team of Andre Levchenko from the Institute for Cell Engineering (ICE) of the John Hopkins Institute, a cell can only make one of two possible decisions when faced with a stimulus. They calculated these decisions to be 0.92 bits of information. However, if, for example, 14 cells group together, they can make up to three or four decisions as a group; that would be 1.8 bits of information. Your Higher Being,

LESSON 3 – SELF-HEALING AND IMPROVING YOUR HEALTH

through your mind and your senses, can perceive up to 11 million bits per second, though it can only properly process 50 bits a second. (Zimmerman, M. -1989).

If we apply these facts to our energy studies, we get a better idea of the difference between the lower beings (lower intelligence) and the Higher Being (higher intelligence). When faced with a stimulus, a cell makes one of two possible decisions: Yes or no, accept or reject. Taken to the extreme, I sicken or I stay healthy. While it is true that the human body is designed to survive, this design does have an expiry date after which our resistance to negative forces (specifically, disease) diminishes.

According to a different study performed by the Commonwealth Scientific and Industrial Research Organization (CSIRO) and published by the magazine Scientific Reports, a human being's natural life expectancy is no more than 38 years, but our advances in medicine, nutrition and life habits have progressively extended it. If we connect this statement with our cells' decision-making capacities, one might think that from the age of 38 our positive cellular responses to disease would not be as powerful as before. Their simple programming (that of the lower beings) makes their responsiveness to negative stimuli (disease) not be as energetic as it used to. Cellular communication will help us positively influence them when they have to make binary decisions.

This is one of the scientific bases that support the convenience of having our Higher Being control or at least hold sway over our cells. Your Higher Being has the power to influence them when they face these binary decisions, and influence them with the parameters we deem necessary in each case. Should you want to gain health, you can send as many energetic messages as possible to help the damaged cells choose to recover instead of letting the negativity win them over and have them drag more cells down with them.

Cancers are born because of DNA mutations, in other words, changes in a cell's genetic configuration. A normal cell lives for a certain period of time and during that time it divides and dies. That is the way of things. A cancer cell "loses" the ability to die and divides endlessly, thus forming tumors (Source: SEOM – Spanish Society of Medical Oncology). The key moment is the binary "decision" made by the cell, its resistance to this negative mutation. That is the key theme of this course: To wield influence from the Higher Being to feed and grant extra strength to the lower beings. In this chapter we will talk about how to overcome diseases by using this means of communication.

LESSON 3 – SELF-HEALING AND IMPROVING YOUR HEALTH

In the previous class I shared two wonderful "all-purpose" exercises that can be applied to most situations in life. If you have a localized problem of any kind or intensity, these two exercises will give your damaged cells the strength they need. Both exercises, that of sending light and drinking light, should become regular exercises for self-healing and preventing disease. Light, its mystery, knowing its essence (that no one has been able to explain) for me is one of the main sources of healing. Light, along with water, is the source of all things. We are surrounded by so much light and so much water we don't often think about how important they really are. When there are droughts, we become aware of the importance of water. Places that are severely affected by them appreciate its importance. The same thing happens with light: regions that are in darkness for several months a year appreciate the importance of light when it finally arrives. I wrote about light and its importance in my book EVOLUTIO. I even described exercises for breathing in light. It is within reach of all. I am going to transcribe a short paragraph from the Mahabharata, written thousands of years ago (it is unclear exactly how many) that sums this up in just a few lines:

"In days of old, all living beings that had been created were sorely afflicted with hunger. And like a father, the sun took compassion upon them. And going first into the northern declension, the sun drew up water by his rays, and coming back to the southern declension, stayed over the earth, with his heat centered in himself. The moon converted the vapors into clouds and poured them down in the shape of water, causing plants to spring up. Thus it is the sun himself, who, drenched by the lunar influence, is transformed, upon the sprouting of seeds, into holy vegetables furnished with the six tastes. Thus the food that supports the lives of creatures is instilled with solar energy. All illustrious monarchs of pure descent and deeds are known to have delivered their people by praying to the sun."

I would like to make clear that I do not believe in the immortality of the physical body and I would never agree with any such claims. The only truth we can be sure of from the moment we are born is that one day we will die. What we described earlier, that when cells don't die they become tumors, could be taken as a sign. The body dies (despite Eduart Punset's wild claim on the Catalan TV program "El convidat" that there was no proof he was ever going to die). My goal with these exercises is to be in complete control of the time we have allocated to live and to live it with as much physical, emotional and mental health as possible.

I don't claim this method to be the solution to so many of the terrible diseases that afflict us. I believe that people who make those claims, guaranteeing to have

LESSON 3 – SELF-HEALING AND IMPROVING YOUR HEALTH

found the way to heal them, are moved by dark interests, enormous egos or deep ignorance. I truly believe in this communication method between the Higher Being and the lower beings as a way to improve or even solve many states, and as such I lay it out before you in this work, but I would never have the arrogance to claim to have found the ultimate solution to disease. What I can emphatically claim is that this inner communication is an efficient self-healing exercise that can also help prevent diseases.

We have already worked on cellular contact. I wanted you to experience this from the very beginning in order to enjoy approaching and working with your lower beings from a different angle. It is good to not focus solely on one method, which is why from now on we are going to explore, through guided meditations, the depths of your innermost self.

Meditations are a vital resource for self-knowledge. For children, fantasizing is natural, but sadly this power is lost as time goes by. The cause of this loss is what the manipulative agents of society and the powers that be call "reality". But they are actually referring to their reality, the reality they impose on us, the jumble of induced desires that busy your mind with trying to obtain them, unaware that induced desires are one of the largest obstacles to achieving inner peace. During meditation, we use the elasticity of the mind to find answers. When we meditate we do not only fantasize, not at all, we re-encounter ourselves and connect with something that yields endless benefits, answers, peace, joy, journeys, rediscoveries, futures, pasts... A well-analyzed meditation holds countless helpful messages in store. Meditation is a means to control the self and get to know it better. In our case, it is a great tool for getting to know ourselves, for approaching and holding sway over our lower beings, our cells.

Through the guided meditations I will describe from this point on, you will travel to spaces of reunion that might resonate within you. And, yes, you will add the wonderful element of fantasy as an additional ingredient. Fantasy is a sorely undervalued human faculty. Its definition speaks volumes: "The human faculty of imagining events, stories or images of things that do not exist in reality or that are or were real but are not present."

We will use this wonderful faculty as a tool for working on our innermost selves. Shall we?

You now have an idea of the beings that live inside you and what your inner world looks like. You also have in your power the information necessary to communicate with them, but let us dive deeper into this communication.

LESSON 3 – SELF-HEALING AND IMPROVING YOUR HEALTH

During this first exploratory trip into ourselves we are going to try to find a deep wound and work on healing it. Perhaps, during the course of this meditation, you might even find clues about the source of this problem. Sometimes these visions appear like messages from your soul to prevent you from repeating the negative patterns that lead to your disease. If these messages do not appear, that does not mean you have done anything wrong, you should never think that.

Before we begin this first meditation, I want you to focus on a physical or emotional pain. You can work on any anomaly no matter how small or superficial it may seem. On a physical level, it can be anything from a simple wound or passing pain to something more complex. You can even work, for instance, on your eyesight, which slowly deteriorates with age, or your hearing, your memory... You can work on anything you want. On an emotional level, you can choose anything related to sadness, anxiety, heartbreaks, anger, etc. If you want, write it on a piece of paper to actively involve your senses. Also, like I indicated in the introduction, keep a bottle of water at hand.

I prefer you focus on working on only one thing. You can always repeat the exercise to take care of other problems. Remember that perseverance is the key to getting results. Performing a self-healing exercise with a generic goal such as "I want to feel well" is less efficient than working on a specific issue. Sometimes it can be hard to recognize, especially on an emotional level, the nature of what is afflicting us, and that makes it hard to have a specific goal in mind, but we have to make an effort to be as specific as possible. This effort for concreteness is already a part of the exercise.

Are you ready? Don't overthink your choice, it can be something small or simple. The goal of this course is to show you the tools you have in your power so that you will learn to be self-sufficient. Define your problem and let's begin. Let's begin with a journey to a wonderful city. The journey to self-knowledge begins now. Your cells are going to embark on a journey to rid themselves of what ails them. You will be their guide, your Higher Being will be their guide.

Let me remind you that meditations are elastic. You should read them and feel them to then later perform them without having to recur to reading, adapting them to your circumstances. These are my meditations as I have experienced them. Make them your own and experience them in your own way.

Welcome to the city of a thousand temples.

LESSON 3 – SELF-HEALING AND IMPROVING YOUR HEALTH

LET'S MEDITATE

You are in a wonderful place on the outskirts of a small walled city from which rise the towers of many temples. It might be somewhere in the Far East. You have decided to embark on a journey without a fixed destination, carrying little with you. It is a journey off the trodden path, far from tourist destinations, you do not want to see what they want you to see. You want to feel, nothing more and nothing less. This is your journey, not their journey; it is for you, not for them. You are not running away from anything; you are looking for something but you don't know what. When you walk through one of the city's many large entrance gates you find yourself on a broad road that looks like a street market. On the floor, hundreds of people offer their wares, fruits, vegetables, handicrafts, anything you can imagine. You walk through it admiring the many things on offer and your steps take you to one of the buildings. It is a sober-looking temple. On its door are beautiful sculpted images of what seem to be dancers. You climb the stairs that lead up to the door, remove your shoes and, with them, the barriers that prevent you from connecting with yourself. It is one of the wonders of temples: they open the soul. A figure carved in black stone of a handsome young man playing the flute indicates that the temple is dedicated to Krishna, the eighth avatar of Vishnu, the beloved Hindu deity with many powers of which you are mostly attracted to those having to do with universal love and the destruction of pain. What better antidote for pain and its causes than love, you think.

When you walk in you see several doors leading to several rooms. You are not in the temple itself, only in the adjacent quarters. You head to one of these rooms and see a large space filled with square columns and countless beds. It looks like a large hospital room. It is a space where boys and girls are treated for their wounds. They are very close to one another. In that space's dome is a small opening through which a tiny ray of light pours in. You walk up to the beds and realize that the patients are representations of yourself; they are your inner children, they are the cells of your body that have been harmed by the problem you are going to treat. The goal you wrote down on a piece of paper. They look scared, fearful, confused and disoriented; they do not know why they are in this place or feel the way they do. To your desperation, you realize they are chained to their beds. You look at the paper on which you have written down the target to heal and you know you are there to alleviate the pain your cells, your lower beings, are suffering and eliminate whatever is causing it. The room is the space that contains your woe and you are seeing your physical state enormously magnified. You determinedly set out to clean that room.

LESSON 3 – SELF-HEALING AND IMPROVING YOUR HEALTH

You look up at the dome and see the skylight is covered with a darkened dirty cloth. When it rains, rainwater pours through that cloth, becoming impregnated with dirt. You think that removing the cloth could help let the light and clean water into the room, but it is too high to reach. You look all over the room for a ladder but cannot find one. You then notice a door at the far end of the hall. You head towards it and open it. To your surprise, it leads into the temple of Krishna. You walk in and feel immersed in love, so much love and protection. You feel well. A flute melody contributes to the general feeling of peace. Leaning against a wall you see a ladder and, thanking Krishna, you pick it up and take it back to your room. "I wish I could make the peace and love I feel in this temple reach my cells," you think. You place the ladder under the skylight, climb up and remove the cloth that dims the light. The effect is outstanding: light floods every last corner of the room, the life of light. You drop the cloth and the dust that had gathered on top of it onto the floor below. You wonder whether it was the lack of bright, clean light that was the root cause of your problem, and you ask yourself who put that cloth up there and why has it been there for so long. Certain memories from the past might come to mind. You look back at your piece of paper and think again about the root cause of those evils and about those memories.

LESSON 3 – SELF-HEALING AND IMPROVING YOUR HEALTH

The dirt that had accumulated on the cloth and the cloth itself litter the floor. They are the remains of your troubles, your pain. Light is pouring into the room but it isn't enough to fill the place with a sense of purity. The skylight lets in the clean air and lots of light, and your cells are beginning to breathe it in and feel relief. Breathe with them. You spot a mass of rain-heavy clouds in the sky. Incomprehensibly, though their density should eclipse the light, this doesn't happen and rain pours into the room as light continues to fill the space. The sunlight and the rainwater reach every corner of the room and all things within it. You and your cells are under a downpour of light and rain. It is amazing to see how the ashen color is draining away from your lower beings as they are drenched in light and water. Their color becomes more natural, the color of your soul. You look at the floor and see the water flowing out of the room through a series of channels, dragging all the dirt away. The cloth dissolves like a sugar cube and is also washed outside. After a while it stops raining. The room is now clean and shiny. Your beings, your cells, look completely different. Their fears and filth are all gone, their general condition has improved in leaps and bounds. The light continues to fill the room and everyone within it. The chains that bound your terrified cells to the beds have also dissolved and disappeared.

LESSON 3 – SELF-HEALING AND IMPROVING YOUR HEALTH

You gather all your lower beings together in that hall and tell them what is behind the door to the temple of Krishna, the temple of love and destruction of disease. You tell them about the flute melody that fills the air and how its vibrations can heal the deepest parts of the self. You lower beings listen closely; the manipulations they were submitted to are now a thing of the past. On their faces you see they have forgotten the memories of pain and the chains that tied them to their beds. They only believe in you because they have seen you cleanse them and fill them with light. They will do anything you tell them in order to fully recover. Gathering and embracing these cells, you guide them to the temple door. Before you walk in, you mentally reread the note on which you described the problem you are trying to treat, you again look at the cells that huddle around you and open the door.

You once again walk into the temple and feel the vibrations of the sound of Krishna's flute. You are reminded of the first great vibration, the one that created the universe, the sacred Om. You once again feel the atmosphere of love that destroys all evil. You find yourself a place, somewhere spacious, and you sit on a carpet with floral motifs. Your lower beings follow you with admiration in their eyes and are filled with the temple's love. You feel their love for you. You feel like the guide of your beloved lower beings and become aware of the reality of your Higher Being, which only desires good. On that carpet, you embrace all your lower beings, filling them with love. The love you feel destroys the disease. Your cells are full of light and water, they are full of life. You then hug them one by one, personalizing your message of healing. You rid them of any remaining ill feeling; these remnants immediately dissolve and disappear. You now better understand the simple intelligence of your lower beings and the importance of communicating with them. With every embrace you make them feel safe, guided, at peace, strong and protected. With each embrace you send a message, you tell them of stars, of nature, of colors, of life. Your fill them with life and health... And you fill them with light, endless light.

You use your fingers to touch, to caress each and every one of your tiny beloved beings.

Fill them with life, love, strength, protection, peace, colors, melodies, light...

Every embrace fills you with waves of information, every embrace is a clue as to the cause of the evil being treated, of the source of that foul cloth. You simply absorb it, but your attention is focused on healing your cells, your little inner children.

You go on embracing, caressing and filling with life, love, strength, protection, peace, colors, melodies, light...

LESSON 3 – SELF-HEALING AND IMPROVING YOUR HEALTH

The faces of your inner children once stricken by this woe are now happy. They play, talk, laugh… They are on the path to recovery. You, the Higher Being, are regaining control over the millions and millions of cells and their simple, pliable intelligence. Krishna is in you and you are in Krishna. You are the temple, and the vibrations of love that flow towards you lead to inner healing.

You stand up and walk towards the door. You are regaining control over your injured beings; you have successfully established a deep connection and you feel better. You step outside and the sun is shining. Its rays fill you with light. You feel powerful; you know you are powerful. You tell yourself you will visit the temple of Krishna often. You must do it because you now know that healing your cells and eliminating implanted memories requires perseverance. You know you will return because you feel complete, loved and powerful in this place.

You leave the temple and walk down the stairs and reach a square with a fountain in the middle. Cool, pure water gushes forth. You walk up to it and touch it. Feel it. It has a special kind of radiance. You fill a bottle with that water and hold it between your hands, filling it with the sensations this place makes you feel (use your bottle of water). You look at the temple and you can still here the enchantingly sweet notes of the flute of Krishna.

LESSON 3 – SELF-HEALING AND IMPROVING YOUR HEALTH

Your fingers send music into the bottle of water. You are sitting on the stairs of the temple, from where you can see, on the horizon, the imposing Himalayas. You feel that the water you are holding between your hands has at some point been a snowflake that landed on those mountains. You feel that this water has the healing power of the stones of the mountains and of the hair of Shiva, through which flow the waters that form the Ganges. You look at it and ask it to help you cleanse the source of your problem. Tell it that when it comes face to face with the damaged cells inside you, those you have healed in the temple of Krishna, you want it to envelop them with its purity and strength and rid them of all evil. And so it shall. Imbue the water with the sense of beauty, peace, harmony, gratitude and love of the place where you are sitting. And now, open the bottle and drink. Give thanks for all the energy that is now going to fill your inner self with life and remove the pain and suffering you might be experiencing. Thank the water that helps you heal.

This meditation is a powerful and flexible tool. I recommend you practice it regularly, first visualizing the problem you want to treat, being as specific as possible and avoiding generalizations. The sensations and messages can help you discover the root cause of your problems.

Well done.

LESSON 3 – SELF-HEALING AND IMPROVING YOUR HEALTH

To summarize this lesson: we have explored a disease in terms of energies, as well as its root causes. We have also explored the decision-making power of cells or groups of cells. Water has, once again, been a source of healing. During the meditation we have practiced connecting with our damaged lower beings and worked on restoring their health from the position of our Higher Being. We have achieved a double objective: on the one hand, we feel physically better, and, on the other, we have reasserted the power of your Higher Being over the lower ones. We have connected with universal energies in this case represented by Krishna. The entire meditation is a channeling exercise that will improve your overall condition.

LESSON 4

Developing Your Gifts and Missions. Self-Knowledge: The Temple of Saraswati

We are born with a wide range of gifts and missions. Sometimes they are readily apparent, and other times they appear in the course of our lives. Each person's circumstances and free will lead to the appearance of new gifts and missions. Self-knowledge and knowledge in general lead to the development of the gifts and missions that are truly our own. Curiosity is the expression of a living soul. Curiosity begets knowledge and self-knowledge.

Some schools of thought claim that gifts are inherited or innate. My humble opinion is that this idea needs fine-tuning. Our souls have been (as I have often said before) through thousands upon thousands of reincarnations, perhaps even hundreds of thousands. Maybe even millions. Every existence, no matter how ephemeral, has involved a learning process experienced through the perspective of the being in which the soul resides. Thus, your soul is an encyclopedia comprising almost infinite knowledge. Your soul remembers each second of its many existences and it has learned from every one of them, even from the negative and harmful ones (that we have probably also have been through). It has learned from all these decisions, experiences, actions... and thanks to that knowledge you are here now, in a new moment. Hence, we all have carry an almost infinite amount of gifts within our souls. For me, it is not simply a matter of who were your parents, grandparents or great grandparents, though of course they help awaken certain aspects. I don't believe much in lineage, among other things because if we have been through thousands and thousands of lives, how many lineages do we really have? I am willing to admit that, in my view, we are born with them, but not from that slightly elitist perspective (let's admit it, perhaps influenced by ego) of thinking that you are somehow special. We are all born with as many gifts as there are gifts in our souls, therefore, thousands. What matters is awakening them. What is right and wrong, social norms, what these determine is worthwhile or not... This is what annuls and hides your energetic gifts from you. I strive for a more fluent connection with the soul to find out what wonders hide within it and how we can use them to lead an existence that is as fulfilling as possible while keeping our future reincarnations in mind.

I am sometimes asked what it is I do, what types of energies I deal with. To this day, I often provide a general answer and say I am simply an energy channeler. Occasionally, if I perceive a genuine interest in the inquirer, I will add that I believe I am an energy enhancer (I will expand on this later). But I should perhaps say what I have just written: "I am a person looking for a more fluent connection with my soul." In this incredibly difficult yet fulfilling connection lies the secret of evolution, inner peace and self-knowledge. The goal of this book is for you to attain that objective, to connect with your soul. Sometimes, our lower beings erect barriers that prevent us from fully connecting with it, as I will now explain.

Our lower beings adapt to and defend the positions we've taken. If we have been "trained" from childhood to be a part of the gearwork of established social norms, our lower beings will want to continue receiving the stimuli provided by said norms. Thus, if they have grown used to burying our natural gifts and connection with our soul under all these implanted social norms (professional success, whims, rules and endless others) they will do everything in their power to stop your Higher Being from changing that situation. To them, it involves investing energy and they tend to avoid that "waste". In this case, we are not talking about single cells, but groups of lower beings that act as a barrier between your Higher Being and your soul. This barrier prevents us from discovering our qualities, potentials and gifts. That, in consequence, can be detrimental to our self-esteem. As a result, our sense of curiosity disappears and is replaced with a litany of "I can't do that", "it's pointless" and so on.

Our mission in this course, and particularly in this lesson, is to break down the barriers that are preventing us from communicating with our souls in order to get to know ourselves more in more depth and increase our will to learn. We are going to teach the lower beings to adapt to the new situation. We are going to experience a battle between the lower beings that have been intoxicated by social norms and your Higher Being, which must take control (take the reins of your life). The time has come to find clear clues about the gifts or missions we are able to develop. Knowledge of our gifts and missions now lies on the other side of that barrier erected by the tainted lower beings. Let's conquer it.

I will now explain what in my view constitute gifts and missions.

LESSON 4 – DEVELOPING YOUR GIFTS AND MISSIONS

GIFTS

A gift is a being's innate ability to develop something extraordinary, if we consider the ordinary to be the level standardized by society. From the energetic perspective, and speaking in general terms, a gift has to do with one's ability to connect with the language of energies that governs the relationships between beings, things and the universal. To have a gift is to have a sixth sense added to the five physical ones. Unfortunately, there are in the world of energies a series of archetypes of what it means to have a gift that we should take a moment to dismantle. It seems like, when it comes to energies, to have a gift is associated with clairvoyance, healing and the power to read energies. In other words: if you are not clairvoyant, a healer or cannot read energies, you do not have a clear-cut gift. Nothing could be farther from the truth. That is an elitist idea that contradicts the essence of the gift itself: humility.

I believe we are all born with gifts or missions, as I have mentioned earlier and repeat because it is important. My view of the energy world, heavily influenced by Hinduism, leads me to believe this is true. Your soul has been through thousands upon thousands of reincarnations and experiences. You have been many things, people, animals, plants and trees; even dirt, air, fire, water, and maybe even light. All these experiences make up your energetic bedrock. Everything you have been through, the mistakes and successes of these thousands of lives, are part of who you are now. These are the foundations of your wisdom. Your soul remembers absolutely everything it has experienced. It has learned a lot and, as a reward for its progress, you are who you are now. How can anyone claim to not have any gifts? Of course you have gifts. You are an encyclopedia containing endless gifts and experiences. The inability to know which of your gifts to develop during this existence lies in your communication with your soul.

There are, of course, many people who don't develop a single gift throughout their lifetimes. These are evolutionary regressions, reincarnations that should be a step forward but, if nothing changes, will end up being a step back. I am not talking about you; you are reading this and other books in order to connect with your being. I am talking about those who get caught up in hatred, extreme attachments, greed, envy; in short, energy poisons. How can someone be in contact with his soul if, for instance, he hates migrants who are running away from hunger? We see far-right parties grow in popularity with their hateful ideologies, their hatred towards all things. Can these people, poisoned to such a degree, develop the gifts contained within their souls in this lifetime? I doubt it. These are not wasted experiences; they are learning experiences for future lives and their souls

LESSON 4 – DEVELOPING YOUR GIFTS AND MISSIONS

will learn from the hatred that this person felt towards others during his brief lapse of existence.

Of course, this is not your case. You are now reading these lines, you have reached out for this book out of a will to discover and improve yourself, you are in touch with your soul. Well, I can guarantee you are already developing your gifts. Do your best to forget the previously mentioned definition of what constitutes a gift; it is much too narrow. A gift is, first and foremost, the ability to transfer energies. These energies have a positive effect on other people. These energetical emissions that have an effect on other people are something you could unconsciously be developing right now. A simple smile or a couple of words can be enough to send a powerful wave of energy to someone. With an attitude to life that might seem natural to you, you could be sending energetical messages that others gather in your wake. With small daily actions, like listening, hugging, talking, laughing... there are so many ways in which you are currently developing your gifts... Think about it, think about your daily behavior and, if you are not already consciously doing this, the first step you should take is to try to make your daily actions broadcast the energy that is in your soul. That is the basis of the gifts: knowing that we emit energy.

Years ago, I gave that gift a name, and I believe the word itself goes a long way in defining the concept. The basic gift is to be energy ENHANCERS. As I shall now explain, being an energy enhancer is the greatest expression of what I believe it means to have a gift, and as you will soon feel, you are one too.

An emission of energy causes a reaction. If one person emits negative energy, whoever received it will feel bad or uncomfortable. If someone emits positive energy, the receptor will feel good. That is the basis of human energetic relationships. Consequently, a positive person's mere presence will make the receptive people around her feel good. Let me underscore that description, "receptive people", as, if we go back to the example of the person who hates everything, it will be hard for him to be receptive, though not impossible.

The energy emitted by a positive person causes a reaction, a stimulus in the recipient. The recipient, for instance, talks confidently and feels good. That is what it means to be an energy enhancer, the greatest gift, that of causing positive reactions in those around us, even when we hardly know them. Have you ever met someone you didn't know all that well who then opened up and shared his concerns, even when these were very personal? Do friends or acquaintances reach out to tell you things, even if they don't expect any advice, just in order to tell you? If so, you have that beloved gift. As you read these lines, you might be asking yourself (or me): what's in it for me? There is not a single answer to that question, but dozens! Human beings want to quantify everything, to have all our activities in balance. Questions without answers seem to not make any sense. Human beings, all human beings, have an ego, and perhaps it is this ego that wants a diploma hanging on a wall to certify we "are" something.

The soul has other yardsticks. It acts in accordance with the experiences it has accumulated through its thousands of lives. If the soul is lucky enough to spend this lifetime in a person who lets her energy reach other people, that person will develop her gifts. This is no small feat; there is nothing more beautiful than helping other with your energy. With this lesson, we are going to try to develop some of the gifts that are inside of you.

Just one note: I guarantee that almost every energetically or socially outstanding person in history and in the present started their journeys by becoming aware of their influence on other people.

I would also like to point out that these gifts aren't limited to the world of energies, not at all. To discover one's gifts is to discover how you send your energy and how others benefit from it. Painting, decorating, building, writing, refurbishing, composing, interpreting, singing, advising, cooking, sewing, drawing, designing, fixing, restoring, talking, helping, caring, listening... These are all gifts that you might already practice or that might be inside of you and now is the moment to proudly give them a chance to shine. But let's take things one step further. We are going to try to make the qualities nestled in your soul bloom so you can make use of them in this existence.

During this chapter's meditation, we will break down barriers that are stopping your gifts from clearly showing themselves.

MISSIONS

I call "missions" the soul's scope for action in this life, actions that will influence others, have an impact on one's own evolution and on evolution in general. The soul, in this existence, is still evolving and, as I have mentioned earlier. It has knowledge and experience that are applicable to this life in order to continue advancing.

Evolving? Advancing? Where to? Well, these are questions all religions and schools of thought grapple with. Some Oriental philosophies believe that the end of the cycle of reincarnation is reached when one attains spiritual freedom (Moksha) and reaches Nirvana. But I believe we should not concern ourselves with this wonderful goal and focus instead on achieving as much

LESSON 4 – DEVELOPING YOUR GIFTS AND MISSIONS

peace and freedom in this life as possible, and we can go a long way in achieving that by communicating with our soul and living in harmony with it. Let us not obsess over Nirvana; it is a process that we can work on in the present through our actions. One can reach the paradox of having the wish to reach Nirvana become so strong it negates the work we can do in the present. I believe we can only achieve freedom in the present moment and through self-knowledge, and I mean in this life! I am talking about liberating developments, little Muktis (liberations) that help our souls advance. I love this life and the opportunities it offers.

So, the final great mission might well be to achieve liberation, Nirvana. In the case of Christianity, which rejects reincarnation (but, oddly enough, does not discard resurrection), the idea of carrying out missions in this life in order to get into heaven also applies. No matter how religious or philosophical you might be, I believe we all share the notion of life missions.

Right, now we have established the endgame, let us focus on our present missions, be they small or large, the bases of this section. Life consists in constantly performing actions. If these actions are carried out in accordance with certain parameters (dharma), you will obtain positive reactions. Small actions produce reactions. Isn't that in and of itself a wonderful life mission? I firmly believe

LESSON 4 – DEVELOPING YOUR GIFTS AND MISSIONS

so. I understand one might want specific instructions, like orders written down on a secret parchment you have to follow... but it doesn't work that way. We have many missions and maybe there is a clue that is common to all of them: to leave a mark on our surroundings, to leave a testimony to our experience so that it will be helpful to others in the future. They are legacies we leave day by day among those near and dear to us and among those who come in contact with you. These legacies are often not recognized as such though they leave a deep impression. This is a common trait of all life missions. This could be another possible definition of life missions: the legacy you leave to others.

Earlier I mentioned inherited family gifts and took a stance slightly against lineages, but I have been able to appreciate the value of having someone close to me who talks about these subjects. This attitude is also another type of mission that falls within our legacies. This mission is to try to provide a different perspective on certain things and share it with those around you. Can you relate to that?

Being aware of the gifts we all have within us makes the missions we have to carry out clearer. A person with the gift of enhancing energies is constantly carrying out his mission, as often as he interacts with the people in his life. I am completely sure that this enhancer has

LESSON 4 – DEVELOPING YOUR GIFTS AND MISSIONS

changed lives almost without knowing it. Isn't that a wonderful mission? Indeed, changing lives by broadening other people's ideas is one of the most important missions possible.

So, let us continue without letting our ego constantly interrogate us about which are our gifts and which missions we are called to fulfil. We will work on developing our gifts and eliminate whatever is in the way of our recognizing them and developing them. This could be another life mission, to develop one's own gifts.

Now that I have exposed my point of view on what constitute gifts and missions and made clear that you are probably already fulfilling them, what is stopping us from finding out more about our capabilities? Several things can get in the way. The way we are programmed from birth by society, as it currently exists, turning its back on contact with out innermost selves; and the education that conditions us to pursue success in financial terms. In short: the social norms that determine what is right or wrong and what constitutes success or failure. This programming poisons any possible fluent contact with the soul. And this is where our old friends, the lower beings, come into play. Cells that have been programmed with these messages and that join together are loathe to change. As we say nowadays, they don't want to leave their comfort zone. Let's remember that their simple intelligence is not well-equipped for dealing with change, which means that when they are intoxicated by social norms that tell you what is right and wrong, they always tend to follow them and send you messages of being unable to change (again). "You don't have any gifts", "don't think about it", "you have to focus on yourself, not on others"... Because these messages come from inside you, you embrace them as your own. Your Higher Being does not impose its will and discards the possibility of change. Do you remember the example of the signs of urgency sent by the lower beings when they are low on energy? Eat, drink... Do you remember how, if they are left to their own devices, you could end up eating non-stop? That is how efficient they are at conforming to the "rules" of society, to ensure you don't become a "rebel".

The inner voice that tells you that you will never be able to discover your gifts, the inner voice that makes you feel like not wanting to investigate, or tells you that you will do it another day... That is the voice of your intoxicated lower beings holding more sway than they should over your Higher Being. The lower beings can make you feel incompetent, lazy, sleepy... Sensations they can easily summon to make you give up. Something similar happens, for instance, with matters as physical as sports, learning a language, dieting... Anything that requires an extra effort will be shot down.

I am sure you must have felt their influence more than once and, coming from inside you, you assumed these messages came from yourself. It is indeed a part of you, but not the part that should be in control of your life.

I think that with this information, the next time you feel some inexplicable urge to not perform an action, you will rebel against it and do it anyway. That at least is the goal of this book. Now it is time to put this into action through meditation.

LET'S MEDITATE

For this meditation, prepare a piece of paper, a pencil and a bottle of water.

We are in the square with the fountain of light-water in front of the temple of Krishna. You drink from it and the jet is so strong the water spills out of your mouth and drenches your clothes and body. It is the water of life and your skin absorbs it as if it were a bath of life. Your interior also reacts to its beneficial properties. You spot a key at the bottom of the fountain. It is small and ornate. You feel it was made for you. You don't know when you will be able to use it, but it is an object that will open or close something important. You tie it to your necklace and go on walking. It is a sunny day and you set out to wander through the city of temples. You walk past the temple of Krishna and it feels like the building is smiling at you, wishing you luck on your new mission. You don't know where you are going; someone is guiding your steps. You head down alleyways bustling with life. They are filled with little shops selling all sorts of products. These roads lead you to a little round square surrounded by buildings. This square also has a fountain in its center. In front of the fountain stands a beautiful temple with ancient walls covered in scars of battles both recent and ancient. There are children playing outside. Three large trees surround the fountain like tall protective warriors. You drink from the light-water that pours from a golden tap and you feel strong and cheerful (now drink the water from your bottle). Next to the door to the temple is a faded painting of the goddess Saraswati, goddess of knowledge, wife of Brahma, the supreme god. You remember seeing her image painted on the walls of a school. There were some words under the painting that said that knowledge leads to freedom. You are standing in front of the temple. You take your shoes off and walk inside. It is quite small inside. It looks like a library with ten tables evenly spread out. Only one of the tables is occupied. You walk up to it and notice the person sitting there is you. You are sitting at the table. You are reading the books some tiny creatures keep bringing to your table. You look sad and confused. It looks like you are searching for answers in these books but cannot find them. The little beings roam the hall and come back with manuscripts you take from them and then cast aside with disappointment. They are how-to books: how to behave, how to acquire good knowledge; how to be a good father, a good mother; how to have a good future, good relationships, a good job; how to be happy, etc. The names of the authors surprise you: they are all marquises, counts, kings, ministers, traders, conquerors, landowners... In short, "successful" people, people who have attained power. You are looking for answers in those books, you are trying to figure out what path to follow, how to leave a mark on others, how to feel fulfilled and discover your gifts and missions. You see yourself reading what the beings hand you and you can tell from your expression that you are not finding any answers. You relate deeply to this image of yourself sitting at the table. You, too, who are also looking for answers, feel straitjacketed by social frameworks that leave you little room to find out who you really are. It saddens you to see yourself this way, you know perfectly well there is a light inside you, but you cannot find what is meant to light it up. Your feeling of disorientation is almost palpable. You remember the words of Saraswati you saw written on the wall and understand that what you are feeling is, in fact, lack of knowledge. You are hungry, hungry for knowledge, for truly knowing yourself.

Suddenly, you recognize those little beings: they are a part of you. They are the feelings that frustrate your attempts every time you try to push the envelope. They are the part of you that has succumbed to the manipulations of the media and society you have been exposed to since birth. It is them, your lower beings. They are the voices that make you stop when you are about to take another direction. They are the insecurity you feel when in the presence of signs from the energetical world. They are the bitter words you hear when you imagine yourself doing things that do not fit within regular social standards. They are the wall that stands between being just another person, like the majority who live with their backs turned to the world of energies, and being a brave person who takes risks to live in harmony with the soul. These imposed social norms, the ones that dictate who you should be, are what is written in the books they are giving you, but you know that the place where you are sitting is a library that has undergone censorship. You will not find the answers to your longing in the books they are handing you. That is why you look so desperate.

Your lower beings are not evil. They are victims. They have internalized a series of codes that make them unmovable in the face of change. You are going to have to confront them if you want to find out more about yourself.

LESSON 4 – DEVELOPING YOUR GIFTS AND MISSIONS

In a corner of the room, flanked by several creatures, is a closed door. Light is seeping in from underneath it, and the light reminds you of the one you saw in the fountain outside. You look at your reflection, still sitting sadly at the table, and you walk to the door. As you approach, the creatures follow you mistrustfully and surround you. You recognize those beings; they are a part of you, they should obey your orders. And yet, they are piling up in front of the door, not letting you through to see what lies on the other side. They are all overly enthusiastically proffering book and papers to you. You keep rejecting them and their enthusiasm borders on violence. They are the same texts you have been reading for years on end at that table, books that don't add anything to the new reality you feel is slowly approaching. These intoxicated beings do not want change. They want you to go on reading and following the books of those in power. But you have seen yourself sitting at that table and you don't want to spend the rest of your life like that. You are saddened by the excessive opposition shown by your lower beings because you love them. You are determined to reach that door; you feel that behind it is something that is going to change your life. Their opposition is fierce and some of your beings start to insult and threaten you. "Who do you think you are?," says one of them. "You're crazy," says another. "Without me you will be nothing," they shout.

"Do what is expected of your age and status," "You're stupid, useless, we are taking care of you," "What will your friends and family think?" The abuse is so hard to take you start to cry and step back as you tell yourself they are right, you are just a normal person, you don't have any powers or gifts, you aren't worth all that much. As the tears course down your cheeks, you look back and see yourself sitting at the table. You have stopped reading the books the beings are handing to you. This time you don't look sad. From the table, she lifts her head and you look proudly at yourself. That look makes you smile. Tears of light pour down from your eyes, the same light as that of the fountain of wisdom you saw on the square. The tears give you the strength you need and when one of the beings forces you to take one of its books, you push it back with strengths you didn't know you had. Two creatures violently rush up to you and you recognize them. They are carrying children's early learning books. You won't let them subdue you and with great sadness, because they are memories from the past, you destroy and eliminate them. The door is getting closer. The beings that accept your strength start to encourage you to go on, they help you and feel liberated. The violent ones that continue to disparage you are painfully destroyed, as you associate them with people and places that influenced your life by cutting the roads that could have led to greater self-knowledge.

LESSON 4 – DEVELOPING YOUR GIFTS AND MISSIONS

You reach the door, put your hand on the handle, look back and see the person who was sitting at the table is now standing right beside you. You see yourself filled with light, joy and pride. She draws so close to you, you become one. You feel her enter you and you feel complete like you had not felt in a very long time. You finally feel your Higher Being is in control of the situation and in connection with the universal.

Before opening the door, you notice a picture on it. You wipe the dust off it and see it is a bright, wise and shining image of Saraswati, goddess of the free flow of wisdom. That is the way you feel: Saraswati is reborn in you with a fantastic hunger to learn.

You open the door and walk into a fabulous, almost endless space; it is the site of universal and eternal knowledge. It is the real great library and here you are going to seek answers, you go to seek your truth, your gifts and missions.

Some kindly lower beings approach you and explain that each and every one of the billions of books contained in here are your gifts and missions. They tell you that during your thousands of lives you have already read hundreds of thousands of them, and now you must choose the ones you wish to develop in this lifetime. And so you shall.

Human beings struggle to accept that we have such a wise essence. All those lives we have lived, all those gifts we have developed, all those missions we have accomplished, all those mistakes we have learned from. All those thousands of existences are comprised within you in this very moment. This moment is a crucial instant. You will feel tiny bursts, maybe only for a millisecond, in which you will become fully aware of the greatness of your soul. This moment is a decisive part of this existence and it is the fruit of the infinite wisdom of your soul. Take a moment, stop reading and feel your soul.

I want to stress, as I have already mentioned, that gifts go beyond the merely energetic; they are actual qualities you posses and that you might not have dared to explore.

With the confidence you now feel, your lower beings are under control and you can count on their unconditional support, you head into this large space. You are amazed at the sheer size of the wooden bookshelves lined with perfectly clean and organized books. The corridors feel like the streets of a beautiful city and the bookshelves like buildings. Willfully lost among all this beauty, one book stands out. You walk up to it and look at it. Your name is written on the spine, as on all the other books, and below it, in small print, is something only you can decipher.

Take it, sit down and discover what is written on that book.

LESSON 4 – DEVELOPING YOUR GIFTS AND MISSIONS

I want you to imagine yourself at this point and let the images the book evokes reach you. Envision yourself performing an action: talking, listening, feeling, helping, empowering, healing, seeing, remembering, teaching, guiding, laughing, cheering, accompanying, curing, writing... Let one of your gifts surface and discover it. You can even recover what you thought was a long-lost childhood dream or a current wish you had ruled out. See yourself, feel the way you are useful to others, the way you bring the best out of them, or how your actions awaken reactions in them...

Decipher the title of your book. Look inside yourself, during this connection you have established with your soul, for clues about your powers. Take your time. It is only one book out of the many thousands that are in your gift library. You can revisit it as often as you want. The door is already open, as the memories that had been implanted in the lower beings that blocked your way are now disappearing.

Write down on the piece of paper you prepared whatever you see or feel or would like. I want you to let your soul fly freely, listen to it. Think about the people in your life, about past, present and maybe future situations, and think about what role you will play in them. Think about yourself too, where you stand with regards to them and to yourself.

LESSON 4 – DEVELOPING YOUR GIFTS AND MISSIONS

If you have managed to decipher the content of the book and write it down on the paper, even if it is a rough draft, we can continue. If you still haven't managed because your mental parameters are still not completely free from the lower beings manipulated by the norms of society, go back to the door and face them down again, grapple with them and fight until you are free from limitations.

Once you have written down the revealed gift, you stand up and put the book back in its place on the shelf. You walk and admire the enormous shelves filled with books of every size and color. You walk through endless corridors, running the tips of your fingers over the spines of the books, until another one catches your eye, attracts you, magnetizes you. It is a little red book with golden embellishments. It mustn't have many pages as it is very thin. You take it and sit at another well-lit table. You open it and see it only contains one page with a single line of text. It says:

NOW IS THE TIME. DO IT.

Close your eyes and picture yourself holding the little red book, analyzing the sentence and what it means for you in this moment. Fight against what remains of the memories that don't let you see what you have to get rid of in order to advance. Look closely at yourself.

LESSON 4 – DEVELOPING YOUR GIFTS AND MISSIONS

Look at yourself as if you were sitting in a movie theater watching the movie of your life projected before you. The actions you are going to perform start to take shape. No one said it would be easy, but you are going to put these things into practice.

Gifts and life missions are sometimes constantly present in our subconscious and maybe these words are a simple reminder of a gift or an action necessary to awaken our gifts. This line encapsulates your new life philosophy. Having gifts and being aware of them is to live with them from the very first moment and act accordingly. Your actions will now be accompanied by that new self-knowledge. If you are an energy enhancer, by being aware of this gift, the good you do for others will be all the more powerful. Anything can be more powerful just by being aware of it. Perhaps at first only a small attitude will change; it is only the beginning.

Lost in thought, but feeling fortunate, you head towards the exit of the wonderful temple of wisdom of Saraswati. You walk through the first room and see hundreds if not thousands of your lower beings fixing up the place; it was a mess after you won the battle against the limiting memories. The first room feels like a completely different space, one filled with light. You walk out onto the square and see a master artist is restoring the painting of Saraswati on the wall next to the door. You look at him, he smiles and so does Saraswati. You tell yourself that maybe that master artist dared one day to paint his feelings on canvas after waging a fierce battle against his lower beings. He was victorious and you can clearly feel his gift, as his painting, our beautiful goddess Saraswati, fills you with infinite strength.

You head to the center of the small square and giving thanks drink once again from the light-water, the same water that gave you the strength you needed during the hardest moments of the fight against your lower beings that did not want to change. Take your bottle of water and drink light-water. As you drink it, imagine the water washing out the last dregs of insecurity left in you. Water is once again your great ally.

Well done.

With this fourth lesson we have explored the notion of gifts and missions. We have also learned the reasons why we don't have access or only have limited access to that wisdom. We have pinpointed the source of the problem, where to find the voice that frustrates your attempts.

You have fought fiercely against the implanted memories. We have worked in the temple of Saraswati and tried to communicate with the soul to find out more about which gifts and missions to develop in this moment in time. We have worked on our self-confidence, detoxified and increased our self-esteem. With a high self-esteem it is easier to discover and believe in our own qualities. Once you have broken down the frameworks that confine you, you are going to discover aspects of yourself you were previously unaware of.

LESSON 5

Working On Your Addictions: The Temple of Hanuman

Addictions are or have been present in almost everyone. We should not only think of addictions as those concerning smoking, alcohol, drugs, sweets... We can also be addicted to people, situations and attitudes, such as the need to be accepted, the need to be appreciated, loved, the need to appear you are something you are not, and of course objects, materialism, the source of endless attachments. The key lies in the word "need", when need clouds and obscures our daily activities.

Addictions are usually born to avoid or bury some form of unease or inner discomfort. This unease, in general terms, is a lack of inner peace and low self-esteem. The energetic solution to addictions involves changing our inner balance.

LESSON 5 – WORKING ON YOUR ADDICTIONS

We are going to work on such a change in the present lesson. During the course presentation, when describing the lower beings as basic intelligences, I enumerated some examples of their behavior. Cells receive impulses when their reserves are low and these impulses are perceived by your Higher Being, which must manage them. For instance, if the impulse is "I am thirsty," the right way to manage this would be to drink water. If the impulse is "I am low on energy," the right way to manage this would be to eat. So, this simple management seems clear enough, but the problems start when the lower beings take control and turn into your spoilt children who whine and whine endlessly for no reason. If you do not accept their demands, the lower beings will do battle with your Higher Being, leading to serious consequences. Those beings, which become stronger and more united when they perceive the weakness of the Higher Being, can send sensations of anxiety, distress, sadness, hunger, thirst, etc. to achieve their goals.

They can adopt the same attitude with regards to alcohol, smoking, drugs and addictions to people, places and things.

If we let the lower beings get used to escaping from unresolved or hard-to-resolve situations by taking substances or clinging to people, situations and things, we are creating an addiction. There comes a moment when your Higher Being succumbs repeatedly to the demands for more and more, and when that happens, we can say you are an addict.

Though our Higher Being is related to the mind, it is not the brain; it goes beyond that. The Higher Being is in your entire being. The brain, understood as the physical place where thoughts are created, is made up of cells just like the rest of your organism. These cells are just as likely to have the same implanted memories as the cells of a toenail. It is normal to feel that the Higher Being is in the mind; it feels like everything happens in there, as if it were the main control station. While it is true that, energetically, channeling the sixth chakra (brow) can help overcome addictions, we are going to take a different approach. Instead of channeling (which we will work on anyway by meditating) we are going to focus on fighting, hand-to-hand, against your intoxicated cells.

Let's go one step at a time. I am going to individually examine addictions to smoking, alcohol and drugs, addictions to food (as it is in high demand) and addictions to situations, people and objects.

SMOKING, DRINKING, DRUGS, GAMBLING...

The cause can be manyfold, from low self-esteem (smoking, drinking or taking drugs to appear more self-assured or mature), to imitating role models or hiding internal energetical problems; our lower beings then tell us to resort to certain actions when we are faced with these situations. The lower beings send messages to your Higher Being about this need as if it were a must, like eating or drinking. The stimuli come in many forms. Some are visual (seeing somebody smoking, seeing a package, etc.) other are catalysts (when the unresolved energy or feeling emerges, you bury it by succumbing to temptation). The Higher Being, defeated and weak before them, surrenders in the face of the false desire that only leads to further desires to consume. We are creatures of habit and continuity takes care of the rest. The lower beings, scarcely inclined to change, go on accumulating excuses to not react.

Giving in to the desire of an addiction aggravates the underlying problem, as it involves taking a step back from the inner harmony necessary to attain inner peace. By smoking, drinking or taking drugs we harm other groups of cells, of lower beings that believe themselves to be despised and abandoned by the Higher Being. It sends the message that we don't care about our physical body and the groups of cells affected feel like children whose parents abuse or abandon them. The disease is then closer.

LESSON 5 – WORKING ON YOUR ADDICTIONS

We enter a vicious cycle of physical and social self-destruction. Something, some unresolved situation, perhaps even something superficial, is makes us feel ill at ease and dissatisfied. We try to fill in the gap left by this lack of peace with the contaminating addiction. Addictive consumption leads to disease, which contaminates our cells and makes us deteriorate in general. Every puff, every sip and every hit drenches our body in filth. Our lower beings, driven to madness by the desire of the addiction, become increasingly stronger and can even convince the Higher Being with myriad excuses to go on consuming. The destruction is mutual and, if the situation gets out of hand, irreversible. Addictions, no matter how superficial they may seem, are stumbling blocks for any kind of spiritual growth. Much of what involves an effort (such as attempts at self-knowledge) is rejected. Addiction, though the addict will rarely admit it, is yet another important hindrance to evolution.

Regaining control over our lower beings and treating the origin of that desire is key to solving the problem. Later, returning to the temple of Krishna can help you heal what has been damaged, and I also recommend using the healing methods involving water we discussed earlier.

FOOD ADDICTIONS

It may seem superficial to dedicate an entire section to food, but it is often the most descriptive example of addiction and the media pollution our lower beings are submitted to. The food market, led mostly by large corporations, has only one goal: to sell. To reach that goal, basic health standards are often flagrantly violated. I don't know many people who are completely free from food addictions; it is hard to escape them. It is a crystal-clear example of media manipulation that touches the very depths of our being, creating the desire to consume something at once.

Sugar, for instance, is one of the panaceas of food manipulation. Sweet was discovered to be strongly addictive a long time ago, and this fact has been mercilessly exploited. Sugar (and all things that contain added sugars for whatever reason) is highly appetizing to humans and if we do not exert a certain level of control, we become addicted and suffer the health consequences that entails. To give you an idea, imagine a 600 ml bottle of coke. It contains 12.5 teaspoonfuls of sugar. 12.5 teaspoonfuls! Imagine eating that many teaspoonfuls one by one. It's insane. Other commercial drinks misleadingly called "refreshments" and even well-known "natural" juice brands follow the same pattern. In sweets and pastries, those amounts skyrocket, and even breakfast cereals, often marketed as healthy, are some of the processed foods with the highest amounts of added sugar. I have included these numbers because they constitute a clear example of what I am talking about in this course. The powers that be, by bombarding you with information through the media, intoxicate you, intoxicate your cells, your lower beings, to make you become addicted to what they are selling. If they have succeeded in your case, your lower beings will tell you to consume these products as soon as possible, and so you do. Every added teaspoonful of sugar in so many processed foods is like taking a drug to temporarily appease your lower beings and harm your health. Sugar can be found in several whole foods, more than enough to cover our daily needs. On average, people in the West consume three times the recommended amount.

But not all food addictions are due to sugar. Salt is yet another example. We often cannot conceive of not seasoning food with salt, despite knowing that too much salt is like poison to the human body.

I have only named two examples, but there are of course many more and on larger scales than salt or sugar. If the lower beings demand this intake and they are left to their own devices, they take control and disease will almost certainly be soon to follow. Eating in excess – and I'm not only talking about sugar – must be treated like an addiction (in most cases). The well-known temptation of opening the fridge is often a response to the demands of our lower beings. Other times, it hides deeper problems. Sometimes, eating can become a reflex just like lighting a cigarette. The truth is that in the West we tend to eat much more than our bodies need, we eat until we are full, which is obviously not right for our health.

And not only in regards to food, but in many aspects of our life, we have lost control over our being. If your Higher Being is in control, the wish to consume will slowly disappear and you will become healthier. Control exercises such as deciding not to indulge these cravings for a period of time are very effective. Overcoming these challenges increases our self-esteem. Once again, water and its positive vibrations will greatly help you.

Jain ascetics are revered to the point that it is an honor to open the door to them and offer them food (but only the allowed foods). However, the food should not be seasoned nor tasty, but tasteless, even when several dishes are offered. Usually, the ascetic Jain will mix it all up to avoid indulging in any pleasures, which constitute a karmic prison. Fasting is a very meaningful and highly valued practice. Isn't it but a way of controlling our inner desires? Our lower beings? Without doubt, it is a gateway to self-knowledge. I must stress just how interesting it is to challenge yourself or give up on certain kinds of food for any period you think necessary.

ADDICTIONS TO SITUATIONS, PEOPLE AND OBJECTS

This type of addictions have a highly emotional component often caused by the social norms that, since childhood, tell you who you should be, with whom you should spend your time and what is the meaning of success. I have already mentioned that one of the characteristics of lower beings is their resistance to change. Once they get used to a situation, they struggle to change. This has its positive sides (if we successfully rid them of implanted memories) and its negative sides (if we spend a lifetime under the influence of social norms and shackled by its parameters of success/failure). Deprogramming is thus necessary to obtain results when dealing with this type of addictions.

By "addictions to situations" I mean being addicted to scenarios which are, and we sometimes even know to be, toxic. What's hard is realizing that they are toxic, as the lower beings cloud your Higher Being's judgement and give a thousand reasons for continuing in the bad situation, including the well-known "the world is against me." Low self-esteem is at play. The good news is that if you are here and you suffer from these situations, that means you are at least aware of it and have therefore taken the first step towards your liberation.

By "addictions to people" I don't only mean to sentimental partners, but even to family members and friends. As in the previous case, these (willing or unwilling) addictions to toxic people annul or cloud our perception of reality. Low self-esteem is the result of this toxicity, though it can also be the cause. Our lower beings drench themselves in dependence and cannot conceive of a situation in which the dominant person is not present. They cannot even imagine laughing without her. Everything orbits that single person and individuality slowly disappears. There are also addictions to people born from admiration to the point that all life decisions, no matter how big or small, are made in order to imitate the idolized person. That is not good at all, as it cancels your individuality. When someone's thoughts regarding a problem do not first and foremost seek answers within oneself but instead turn to someone else to decide for them – I believe this is being addicted to a person. I have seen many cases of addictions to people that end up leading to important set-backs, even in energetical terms. The disciple tries to imitate the guru as much as he can, when the guru's role should be to shed light on the disciple's inner self to help him reach his full potential. Sometimes this type of addictions border on caricature, such as when fans adopt a celebrity's wardrobe, mannerisms and even appearance (to the point of resorting to plastic surgery!). The purpose of these addictions is clearly to escape being oneself. There are other serious situations in which addictive attachments can lead a person, after her death, to not continue her evolutionary path and instead cling to the energies or objects belonging to the idolized person. These cases are usually limited to some extreme types of emotional and familial relationships.

While talking and learning about energies with a person I considered to be very intelligent (not because he isn't anymore, but because we lost contact), I realized he might be addicted to his guru. As he spoke, and he spoke of many interesting things, he mentioned him every time he made a statement. I noticed how before saying anything unusual, he would always make clear that he was quoting the guru. At one friendlily heated point of the debate he reprimanded me for having different sources of learning and beliefs. I told him that Swami (translated from Sanskrit) means owner of oneself, which is why it is one of the most beautiful words I know. To me, the word Swami encapsulates individual freedom and the power to change in the face of new knowledge. He became thoughtful, was about to say something, and ultimately stayed quiet. I think he was going to say something his master would have said but stopped himself.

By "addictions to objects" I mean the unhealthy attachment to any material object. This exaggerated attachment is a dangerous energetic poison that can lead to selfishness, greed, self-importance, etc. The lower beings react to being separated from something as if they had lost something without which they cannot be happy. The desire to amass objects is a craving that always leads to dissatisfaction. When something comes into our possession, we feel fleetingly happy, but this happiness just as quickly disappears as we start to wish for something else. Being overly attached to objects from the past (memories) can also be dangerous. It stops us from entering new stages in life. It is an ongoing reminder of an idealized time. I wrote in EVOLUTIO about the dangers of dying while still being addicted to objects and harboring extreme attachments. A person who reaches the end of his days in this physical stage of life might have tied his soul to certain objects (his possessions) and can end up trapped in them by clinging onto them. His intoxicated soul will remain on this plane of existence watching how all the things he once possessed slowly pass into the hands of others, increasing his anger. Many cases of negativized spirits in houses are due to this. They cling to the walls and attack the new owners in any way they can, because they believe these people are occupying their home. These cases are unusual, but certainly possible.

Now we have outlined these three kinds of addiction (I apologize for over-simplifying) we can also observe that they all steal our time, one of our most prized possessions. Any addiction steals time, even addictions to food, because the life of a food addict tends to be shorter and of lower quality.

To face these addictions one needs to be very strong, aware of one's own Higher Being and its strength in order to defeat the influences that impregnate the lower beings, eternalizing these attachments. The lower beings don't so much cause addictions as sustain them. Your inner strength, which is tied to your Higher Being, will help you overcome any type of addiction. No one said it was easy, but it is in your hands.

Giving up on certain things for a limited time, as I have mentioned, is an important tool... These self-control exercises can help you measure you level of addiction, and also help you learn to control them and even get rid of them. It is simply a matter of choosing something you are attached to, be it eating, social networks, smoking, drinking... and make do without it for a certain period, as long as you think necessary. During that time, you are going to feel the pressure exerted by your lower beings, urging you to break your promise to yourself. This will help you diagnose just how addicted you are and will put you on the path to detoxification. The results are usually very positive. Self-esteem goes up and a greater control is exerted over the lower beings. To quit an addiction, it is often recommendable to do so gradually.

Most of the time, this will at least help you gain control over your actions. I encourage you to set yourself a small goal and start working on it right away. It will help you with the following lesson.

I always recommend complementing your work on addictions of any kind with spending time in nature, exercising, drinking water and its vibrations, and going out to breathe in the light.

Before we begin the next meditation, I would like you to take a deep, honest look at yourself and write down the addictions you think you might have. Then choose the one you want to work on. Maybe you have already committed to giving up on something temporarily, as I previously suggested. If so, you should work on that addiction during this exercise. The bottle of light-water must always be close at hand, along with the piece of paper indicating the addiction you want to tackle.

LET'S MEDITATE

You have just finished drinking from the fountain of light that is in front of the temple of Saraswati. The seed of new knowledge has just been planted in you. On the right-hand side of the temple is an arch that leads to a less well-known part of the city. The streets are narrower and almost devoid of sunlight. Even so, the streets are filled with people talking, shouting, running, offering their wares...

At the end of the street is a large door, the entrance to some lofty space. Around the door are several pictures and colored sculptures of scenes featuring strong half-monkey, half-human warriors. You walk through the door and see a 15-meter-high statue that greatly attracts your attention. It is a towering figure of Hanuman, the monkey god, the great protector and defending warrior. The hands of Hanuman are tearing open his chest, revealing the figures of Rama and Sita, thus showing us who inhabits his heart. Hanuman's strength has always been at the service of what is good, true and peaceful. You feel your chest vibrate as you look at that figure. You recognize the strength within you and you are going to break free from the shackles of addiction. Behind that figure is a long staircase leading up to the inner part of the temple. You are about to enter the wonderful temple of Hanuman.

Climbing the stairs requires effort; there are hundreds of steps. As you climb, monkeys observe you and try to snatch things visitors usually carry. You see another large statue of Hanuman at the top of the stairs, this one showing you the palm of his hand. You interpret this gesture not as an indication to stop, but as a protective gesture that dispels your fears. Don't be afraid.

LESSON 5 – WORKING ON YOUR ADDICTIONS

When you reach the feet of the towering figure, you feel protected and devoid of fear. It feels like Hanuman won't let you carry any fear into the temple. You feel free to search for and work on ways to remedy your addictions. With his strength, Hanuman is silencing the lower beings that incite you to succumb to temptation. Now that your lower beings are willing to listen, you can enter the temple.

You take off your shoes. The door is small and the room on the other side is austere. There are several people in the room. Some are talking jovially, others are praying, other are beggaring and some are by themselves, far from the rest, standing alone in a poorly-lit corner. You feel the need to approach one of them because, though you struggle to admit it, you see a bit of yourself in them. She is sitting on the floor, covering herself with an old blanket. When you look her in the eye, she averts her gaze and covers herself with the blanket. In her eyes you have seen fear, anger, arrogance and degradation. You speak tenderly to her, you tell her you have come to help, and she answers from under the blanket that it isn't necessary, she is perfectly fine, she can control whatever it is that can harm, if there even is such a thing. She lowers the blanket and you see she looks younger, more beautiful and positively radiant. You see your reflection looking outstandingly perfect. "You see?" she says, "I am fine. And you?" You are confused because this isn't the

LESSON 5 – WORKING ON YOUR ADDICTIONS

face you had seen a moment ago, but you accept it and decide to move on. She is looking at you but you notice something change. Her eyes become dimmer, her skin darkens, she coughs, gets dizzy, her hair becomes tangled and loses its color, her features fade and her skin clings to her bones. Her hands desperately clutch something viscous, heavy and dark. She has turned back into what you had originally seen. Shen quickly covers herself with the blanket again.

You are standing in front of a part of yourself. You are looking at a group of lower beings clinging to the addiction you want to remove from your life. You hear a voice. Someone in the temple is telling you about Hanuman and his devotion to Rama and his spouse Sita. You listen to the story as if in a trance. Rama is the god that represents all virtues: goodness, piety, bravery... His spouse, Sita, is the source of inner peace. Ravana kidnapped Sita, stealing Rama's precious treasure (his partner and peace).

The speaker goes quiet for a moment and looks at the figure that remains practically still under the blanket. His silence clearly signals that the inner peace of your lower beings has been kidnapped by the demon of addiction.

He continues the story. Rama gathered armies to free Sita and was lucky to meet Hanuman on his way. Hanuman,

LESSON 5 – WORKING ON YOUR ADDICTIONS

who is strong enough to lift mountains, freed her from the clutches of Ravana. Pointing at the center of your chest, he whispers: "Hanuman is in here." You approach you lower being, embrace her with infinite tenderness. You gently remove the blanket that covers her. She resists but ultimately your love makes her give in. Her figure, your figure, is almost entirely covered in the dark liquid that oozes out of the object she is holding and you start to clean it up. You delicately but firmly tear off the viscous layers and deposit them in a bucket beside you. These layers are the results of your addiction. As you remove them, you see your beautiful and thankful self slowly emerge. Your physical interior, your lungs, your liver, your heart, your brain... all your organs slowly release the contaminating paste that you remove with all your love. But her hands still firmly cling onto the object of addiction. It is now a dirty crystal ball with something inside of it. Look at it, look at the root of your addiction. Set aside your ego and look at it. Only when you see it, understand it and forgive yourself for it, will the viscous matter that is stealing your life stop gushing forth from the ball.

Observe the ball...

Don't blame others... observe.

Don't be afraid, Hanuman is with you, you are Hanuman and you will rescue Sita, your inner peace.

LESSON 5 – WORKING ON YOUR ADDICTIONS

Observe while you go on cleaning and depositing all the negativity in the bucket. You notice the ball is now a bit smaller and the eyes of your lower being are shining a bit more brightly.

Observe, look for the root of the problem while you clean your being.

You can still feel occasional bursts of loathing towards you. It feels as if two personalities are fiercely fighting within. At times it feels like the battle is lost, but the strength of Hanuman, the strength of your Higher Being, successfully repels the attacks of your addiction one after the other. You understand that you won't have inner peace until you are rid of this viscous matter. And that is what you want, to be at peace to pursue your goals, to have the addiction stop stealing your time and health. You are defeating it; facing it is to begin to defeat it.

In your hands is the bottle of light-water you filled at the fountain in front of the temple of Saraswati. You are going to use the light contained within its atoms to clean and wash the dregs out of your being. You offer her the bottle of water. She drinks, you drink, and she feels, you feel, the atoms of light pouring into you and lighting up the darkened places. You have the power to see them dissolve and remove the grime of the addiction from the walls of your inner organs. As the grime melts it drops and disappears. Contained within it are the false

LESSON 5 – WORKING ON YOUR ADDICTIONS

pleasures of addiction, whichever it may be. You drink and the vibration of the wisdom of Saraswati makes you see that there are many ways to solve what is contained within that crystal ball. You have discovered that you have a number of gifts and missions that are waiting for you, and without the burden of darkness, you are going to carry them out with renewed strength. Hanuman, the higher strength, is completely submitted to your Higher Being. You feel invincible. It will not be easy, but you like to feel yourself gain control over your being. You are shedding things you once thought essential.

You have taken the first big step towards overcoming your addiction; you are now stronger and must go on cleaning its remains. You must make that crystal ball lighter; it is still too heavy. With perseverance, you can do it. There will come a moment when any time a lower being tries to tempt you with an addiction, you will react with repulsion and even indifference. At that moment, you will know yourself a bit better and you will have pushed a time thief away from your being.

You both stand up and head towards the exit. With every step you both draw closer to one another until merging into a single body. You have recovered an isolated part of yourself.

You walk out of the temple and in front of you are the hundreds of steps leading down towards the exit. This is how it is going to be from now on; once you have started to regain control over your being, everything becomes easier, like walking downstairs. You must be careful not to stumble. You must be careful not to get distracted when placing a foot on a new step. You must make sure nothing ever steals your time again. As you walk down the stairs, you think about the time, effort and health invested in the addiction you are starting to overcome. From now on, your days are going to be longer and all those reclaimed hours are extra hours of life. This new time you are already benefitting from opens up before you like a space of infinity possibilities in which to do the things you have always wanted or even, as you discovered in the temple of Saraswati, to develop your potentials, your gifts and missions. But right now, enjoy walking down these steps of liberation. Paradoxically, the more time you invest in loosening your bonds, the more time you will have for yourself.

At the feet of the towering figure of Hanuman, you feel thirsty and drink light-water filled with simple things. You tell yourself that perhaps things are much simpler, and that we humans needlessly get ourselves into useless and even toxic situations. You look at the water, its humility, so present everywhere and therefore so undervalued on account of its abundance. And yet, so craved for when it's missing.

LESSON 5 – WORKING ON YOUR ADDICTIONS

You drink, it cleanses you and you are thankful.

Once you have passed the towering figure of Hanuman, you turn back smiling at him and your eyes well up with emotion. It is one of the most beautiful feelings, one of those that come over you when you smile happily.

Visit the temple of Hanuman to become aware of the strength of your Higher Being. Hanuman is the warrior of your inner peace and the guardian of dharma, of correct behavior. His strength is your strength and what tempts and intoxicates you is Ravana kidnapping your inner Sita. When you feel in danger of relapsing, try charging water with the methods we have learned and, as you drink, visualize it cleansing every last corner of yourself.

Well done.

With this fifth lesson we have outlined three types of addictions, and we have defined the process that leads to addictive desires. Discovering or getting an idea of the root cause helps overcome the addiction. We have worked in the temple of Hanuman, the almost infinite strength that is within you, and discovered the effect addictions have on our interior. We have cleaned our interior, working on the root cause and effects of the addiction.

LESSON 6

Overcoming Fears Caused by Ego: The Temple of Kali

This is the hardest lesson of the entire course, the one that will make you feel the most uncomfortable, but perhaps the one that will lead to the deepest self-knowledge. Your lower beings, infected with ego, are going to forcibly try to manipulate you and make you give up on this work of self-improvement. When someone denies having an ego, that is the greatest proof that he actually has one. Few, almost nobody, can truly escape its effects. This lesson is tough because it involves undermining the foundations of the reasons for which we do the things we do. It involves casting a critical eye over everything we have done so far. It involves dismantling structures. But we will not look back as if time lived were time wasted; everything you have been through in your life has led up to this moment. It has been necessary.

We, and therefore our lower beings, have been programmed from birth to be loyal to the establishment, to what is supposedly correct, to the artificial values of success, to the canons of happiness, or rather, false happiness. This programming has been constant and powerful, and like an extreme drug, it binds you to behaviors accepted by the establishment. If you stray away from them, the consequences are akin to those of trying to quit drugs; you suffer a form of withdrawal syndrome. A consequence of this withdrawal is fear. You might be surprised to learn that many fears are born because of ego.

Before we begin, I will try to define the concept of fear on an energetic-spiritual level. Most of the time, fear is a reaction your lower beings announce to your Higher Being when faced with change of the possibility of change. Fear is a weapon of ego to avoid changes that involve making any amount of effort. The lower beings believe it dangerous and a huge investment in energy to veer away from the establishment. The establishment, what is considered socially correct, is what society and its norms and forces of consumption want you to be, the ideas they have implanted in your mind, in all of our minds. All it takes is a quick look at the idealized versions of life shown in commercials. If we are not attractive, smart and rich; don't own a spectacular home or high-end clothes; or don't have spectacular bodies, cars, friendships, meals, holidays... We don't have a right

LESSON 6 – OVERCOMING FEARS CAUSED BY EGO

to be happy. That is the message the media constantly bombards us with. When your Higher Being wants to take control of your lower beings, they react by sending signals, energetic messages in the face of the change you are about to carry out. If said change involves rebelling against these models of false happiness, the contaminated lower beings react with severity. One of these reactions is fear. The lower beings' control spreads to the mind and that is where the arguments for boycotting change are born. We once again find ourselves hearing sentences I have repeated several times, such as "What will they say if I do that," "I cannot," "I am not ready," "I am not worth it," "What will they think," "I'm too shy to open up to others," "They will think I'm crazy," "What will become of me without him/her," "They won't love me anymore," "I will lose my friends and loved ones," and many more. These thoughts are typical of people who live under the yoke of their lower beings. In short: it is fear of change born from fear of losing love, friendships or status. You feel fear whenever you consider making a change, right?

Ego is behind this fear of change. It created it as a weapon to defend itself, and it is the consequence of fears that often don't seem to have anything to do with the change we want to make. Your lower beings are impregnated with the ego that has been planted in you and that reminds you that you need other people's approval in order to be happy. You need to be and have what you are told. Without that approval, an abyss seems to open up under your feet. That abyss makes you feel fear. It goes like this:

*YOUR EGO INSTILLS FEAR
TO PREVENT CHANGE.*

Your ego does not want change, it does not want a personal development that connects you with your soul and changes your life because that would "only" involve getting inner approval and not social approval. It is misleading and powerful and it will try to boycott any attempt at change through your lower beings. That is why ego is the enemy of personal development.

A life without change, without risk, can hardly be a fulfilling life. Small and large rebellions make these changes possible. Fear blocks the decision-making process, it oppresses and leads to disease. Ego impregnates your lower beings and will place stumbling blocks on your way to completing or even starting a project or a relationship. Ego is very smart and when it gains ground inside you, to stop you making any changes, it engenders more and more fears so you will give up on the idea. Fear of commitment, of getting sick, of failure, of loneliness, of separating, of death, of abandonment, of going out, of driving, etc. are some typical examples. It is interesting to note that some of these fears are paralyzing,

LESSON 6 – OVERCOMING FEARS CAUSED BY EGO

a word synonymous with "block". Fear paralyzes and makes you sick, because it brings with it anxieties, low self-esteem and even depression when you realize that, sometimes, you cannot even leave the house. The memories contained within your cells due to the constant bombardment they have been submitted to since birth are the foundation on which your ego is erected. That is why this lesson is so hard, because we are going to deconstruct much of what has been planted inside us. You are going to have to question things you took for granted in order to create new memories and eliminate the old ones.

I imagine it must be surprising to learn that ego is behind our fears. I will repeat it as often as necessary. An argument against this statement is that if someone puts fear aside and embarks on a new project, ego can also be the driving force behind this decision in order to help you succeed and thus obtain social success. This is partly true. It means you once had fears but successfully defeated ego, dispelled your fears and created a project. But if you have defeated ego, you will know what to expect moving forward and will be ready to face it. Ego will cunningly tell you to make a deal so it will help you reach your final goal: success. To fall into this trap would be to start over again. If you have done inner work, the goal of this new project, be it financial or emotional or of any nature, will not be to prove something to others,

LESSON 6 – OVERCOMING FEARS CAUSED BY EGO

but to be happy and coherent with yourself. You will be implementing what you have learned. But never make a deal with ego!

Now we have explained what is often behind these fears and the mechanisms employed by ego, it's time to get to work.

It's just you and me now, face to face. If you really want to work on some fear in depth, answer this question with your soul: How much of what you do or how many of your desires are motivated by ego? By the acceptance of others? By social success instead of personal success? By proving to others you are successful? The first answer usually falls along the lines of: I only want peace, happiness and luck for my loved ones, health, etc. But I'm asking you to go beyond that and analyze whether that imagined world of happiness, peace and luck includes the parameters of the rules of society and consumerism, especially with regards to social recognition or what society would consider success. I want you to make an effort and ask yourself whether your goal of dispelling your fears is a goal free from outside manipulation and ego. As I mentioned earlier, ego offers up deals when it is cornered, and right now you are cornering it. It pretends to be your ally. "We are going to make your dreams of peace come true and conquer your fears," it tells you. "I will take you to the next stage, help you through it, make sure you have fun and succeed," it insists. "You will be able to show others you are a different person," "You will have access to the pleasures you have so often seen in your acquaintances' photos of journeys, restaurants... You will show them how your efforts have led you not only to make it but surpass their own achievements," it claims. If so, ego has slithered into your wish to conquer your fears. It will feel like you have defeated it, but it will have simply adapted to change. Fear, in this case, has gone into hiding and lies waiting for its chance to return.

It is very difficult, almost impossible to act without the intervention of the egos that have been planted in us by the consumerist laws of society and, consequently, of what is considered social success, which is usually uniform. Our job is to rid ourselves of them as much as possible. With the work you have done so far, you will see that every aspect of ego you banish from your mind and daily life will take a part of your fears with it. This process will bring you closer to having moments of inner peace and, therefore, be less afraid.

The process consists in identifying and destroying egos. Cleaning up small aspects of your life and behavior that have been influenced by said ego. Trying to attack fear as a whole is very difficult, which is why it is probably a good idea to wear away at it through small successive battles. Every time you destroy a part of your ego, no matter how small, you will feel a bit more liberated. You must imagine this liberation like a broken chain giving you greater freedom. The material those chains are made of is fear. This attitude will make you be extremely careful moving forward, you will be on guard to make sure ego does not also start stealing your time.

I will give you an example: a person who is afraid to leave her partner. Her lower beings tell her constantly that without her partner, without his protection, her life would fall apart. She would not find a job, she would lose shared friendships, she would lose her family's love or part of it, she might even lose her social comfort and status. Then the recriminations begin: "You are nobody by yourself and you won't achieve anything," the lower beings say. She doesn't feel love anymore, but she keeps up appearances. This person is afraid of change, afraid of moving on, and she prefers to remain blocked and miss out on living new experiences. Fierce self-criticism (the only kind that makes you realize this is all rooted in ego) proves that this person wants to stay in her comfort zone, even when it is a false one.

She knows that if she would lose her friends, then they are false friends, and she accepts this (the ego that wants to be socially appreciated).

She knows that if a part of her family resents her decision, it will mean she would never have been able to count on them or trust them in the face of any important problem, that their love is not real (the ego that wants to be loved at all costs, even at the expense of giving things up). Another part of her family will certainly give her the support she needs.

She knows that she might suffer financial difficulties if she goes her own way, and she will have to tighten her belt and lower her standard of living. The ego of social shame rears its head.

She will have to find a job, any job, to cover her expenses (ego can lead to shame and make you feel deeply sad in an attempt to make you quit your job and return to the relationship).

"Who will take care of me if I am sick?" (ego can blackmail you and even conspire with the mind to make you believe you are sick).

She will not be able to go on holiday nor take selfies in stunning locations. She will not be able to go to restaurants nor buy expensive clothes.

The decision this person has to make is very important. To keep up an artificial life without love in order to appease her ego or to be free. If this person works hard

LESSON 6 – OVERCOMING FEARS CAUSED BY EGO

on every one of the dimensions of her ego, the fear to decide to start a new stage will slowly fade away. Her lower beings, contaminated by ego, are controlling her Higher Being by sending messages of immobility and stasis. The cellular memories are activated.

If she can overcome her fears, defeat her ego and decide to break up the relationship, a wonderful new phase opens up before her. She will be acting coherently. She will have learned that most of the things that sustained the relationship were false, underpinned by ego. She will not miss the comfort (she will find a new, more fulfilling comfort) nor the false friends she had to put up with in supposedly fun gatherings. She will not miss many possessions, which she will come to see were actually unnecessary. She will not waste days and years of her life thinking about how to appear agreeable to others, how to be admired, or even envied. Here is yet another example of time thieves. This person will realize just how much time she invested in maintaining something she didn't really care about. This person is on the road to liberation. Then something wonderful will happen. Only the people who are really valuable to her soul will remain in her life and... she will meet new people who find her attitude to life attractive. People who are steeped in ego will not be interesting to her in the least. She will be free. Like-minded people will enter her life, no doubt. I guarantee that this liberation will make transitioning to a new stage much easier.

Another example: the fear of going out or driving. Nobody would say these things are caused by ego, but they often are. Sometimes, the lower beings poisoned by an ego unwilling to change produce this type of fear when change is imminent. If this is your case, ask yourself when you started to feel these fears, what projects or important decisions you had to make. The answers might surprise you.

Ego does not always beget fear, it can be responsible for all sorts of actions. Perhaps there is a part of ego involved in the fact that you are now seeing or reading me. For many years I have avoided being photographed. I felt comfortable on the radio because that way my image was kept hidden. Recently I decided to appear publicly on social networks. My reasoning was that my message would be clearer if the person receiving it can see who the message is coming from. So far so good, but what if my ego was behind all this? What if it was my ego that led me to talk about subjects as if I were some sort of master with answers to every question? I will take it a step further. What if it is my ego that is making you feel like you should support my decision? If you say, "No, it's not the same, it is good to see you physically to better understand the message...", my ego feels comforted and

LESSON 6 – OVERCOMING FEARS CAUSED BY EGO

it might even be my ego that is making me write this paragraph to garner support... Complicated, right? So that's ego. It is cunning and devious. It tries to always be present by wearing a thousand disguises.

Some very difficult situations are caused by the memories and egos contained within the lower beings, so difficult in fact they are hard to put into words because they could easily be misunderstood. Emotional blackmail, for instance, is usually the result of a very dangerous kind of ego. The fear of losing something makes us fall deeper and deeper into extreme situations often having to do with health. What's dangerous is that, sometimes, what starts out as an illusion ends up becoming true. Ego makes us call out for attention out of fear of losing something, or the fear of losing something leads our ego to make us call out for attention in any way possible. These are special cases but very real. I have already warned you that this lesson might stir things inside you and might even be controversial.

Let's work on our egos, not only to dispel unnatural fears but to stop them from coming back.

And now, for the meditation, choose an ego and a fear. Try to discover connections between them (it isn't easy). As I said earlier, ask yourself when a fear appeared and what changes you would like to make. Remember the formula:

LESSON 6 – OVERCOMING FEARS CAUSED BY EGO

YOUR EGO INSTILLS FEAR TO PREVENT CHANGE.

The battle against ego lasts a lifetime. This is the most important exercise in self-criticism we can do and the one that requires the fierccst and most destructive inner struggle. That is why we are going to turn to Kali, the energy of Shiva and the goddess that destroys evil and demons (in this case, inner demons). Kali faces the worst aspects of every one of us and that is why her destructive capacity is so high. Shiva represents destruction and creation, which is exactly what we want, to create a new way of being. Kali is the most destructive aspect of Shiva. She will help us.

If you have detected some form of ego, you can write it down (I like writing things down as it adds a physical dimension to the exercise) and we are going to try to work on that aspect of yourself. Keep the bottle of water always at hand.

LET'S MEDITATE

You walk out of the temple of Hanuman. You have left the towering figures behind. There is a narrow alleyway leading to a broad road. You feel compelled to walk down it and so you do. It if full of people. You once again lose yourself in the life, sounds, smells and chaotic charm of the day-to-day bustle. To a side, on a stone wall, are seven running faucets. People line up in front of them and when it is their turn they perform a beautiful ritual. First they greet it and show thankfulness, then they soak their hands, face, head and even their arms and legs. Before they leave, they once again express their gratitude.

Above these faucets is an inscription:

"ALL WATER IS THE GANGES"

Somebody once told you that the water of the Ganges comes from heaven. It pours through Shiva's hair and every lock turns into a stream that ends up forming the holy river. If feels like Shiva the destroyer and creator and you, on your quest to destroy things inside you and create new ones, are standing face to face.

When it's your turn, you perform the ritual with intensity, as if it were something you had been doing your whole life. The waters of the Ganges clean and bless your skin, they seep deep inside you and clean and bless your soul. It feels like the heavier karmas dissolve and disappear. When you give thanks before leaving, you look to the sides and exchange knowing glances with the people who performed the ritual at the same time as you. Their eyes are full of joy, as are yours because you are getting to know yourself.

LESSON 6 – OVERCOMING FEARS CAUSED BY EGO

You continue to walk along that large street, and the hustle and bustle never ceases. You realize you are grinning and you think about how you have changed and how your loved ones will react when you return and they notice your new attitude. You only wish to make them feel even a small part of what you are feeling right now.

Stalls line both sides of the street. They are overflowing with objects, fruit, necklaces and multicolored flower garlands. They are offerings for the temple you can discern at the end of the street. You buy an offering and head towards the entrance. You try to store all these feelings inside your mind so you will be able to share them when you go home, but there are so many...

Once at the door, the disturbing image of Kali – naked, blue, with eyes wide open and a long red tongue hanging from her mouth – makes you hesitate and wonder whether you should go in. Her hands are covered in blood. She holds a machete in one hand and a severed head in another. She is wearing skulls around her neck... You don't know whether this is the place for you. You feel uncomfortable. You feel afraid. But you take your shoes off and walk in, determined to pay your respects.

The place is only lit up by torches. There are several paintings of Kali. In some she looks kind and caring; in others she looks terrifying. But in all of them those big eyes stare at you wherever you go. You decide to put your concerns aside and sit on the floor in a corner of the temple, in front of a towering figure of Kali that observes you, scrutinizes you. You feel her strength within you. You start to hand her the offerings, but you realize something is not right. Those eyes are boring deep inside you, as if uninterested in the effort you are making. And then you start to cry.

Kali feels no compassion for egos that cause fear and blocks, she has no patience for anything negative. For her, there are no excuses. Her mission, when somebody truly wants to move forward, is to penetrate them and mercilessly destroy them. The pain this can entail is a secondary matter. She has located and cornered an ego, the same one you located, and her eyes are asking for permission to dive into you and destroy it. Kali wants to decapitate the ego that is causing your fear and add its skull to her necklace.

You ask her to give you a minute to think about that ego and the fears it awakens in you. It is precisely those fears that make you hesitate and you understand that it makes sense, that fears are your ego's defense mechanism. You look at the piece of paper on which you have written the aspect of yourself you want to work on. You nod and determinedly say goodbye to it...

Your tears don't placate Kali. You see her through them, blurry but looming. You are ready to let her take action and help you eliminate that ego and fear you have written down. And then, in the moment of acceptance, Kali, without ever taking her eyes off you, changes her expression and you recognize features that are similar to yours, until she turns into you. The sound of drums and bells fill the temple. You also hear a mantra that you don't quite understand. Om Kali Mahakali... You can only discern that sentence and you grasp onto it.

OM KALI MAHAKALI
OM KALI MAHAKALI
OM KALI MAHAKALI

You interpret the mantra as a sign of permission for Kali to destroy whatever is stopping you from advancing. You repeat it, granting her permission.

OM KALI MAHAKALI
OM KALI MAHAKALI
OM KALI MAHAKALI

Kali is in you, you recognize yourself in her, she looks into your soul and your soul smiles. Kali surrounds your ego, your fears, and sets our to destroy them.

OM KALI MAHAKALI
OM KALI MAHAKALI
OM KALI MAHAKALI

LESSON 6 – OVERCOMING FEARS CAUSED BY EGO

Kali can now see your fears. She sees them contaminating your lower beings. Kali sees that those fears are the tools your ego uses to paralyze you and prevent you from rebelling. The trap set by your ego to creates fear and submit you so you won't move forward. Think about that one specific fear and ask Kali to destroy it and everything associated with it. You see yourself, you see the shape of your false being, you see what others want you to be. And you see the way it fools you and makes you feel afraid to hold you back. You draw nearer and see that it is in fact not you, but a mask, and behind the mask is a dark and gloomy creature. You recognize it. It is the being that has so often manipulated you; it is a negative implant. You look at Kali, your eyes shine after having discovered the root of your fears. Kali, quick and ruthless, decapitates and destroys it, eliminating it.

> *OM KALI MAHAKALI*
> *OM KALI MAHAKALI*
> *OM KALI MAHAKALI*

You feel the light of fear inside you. The light of fear destroys what has been implanted. Your fear disappears and you let Kali take control. She destroys and from that destruction you appear, clean, filled with light, happy and content about having gotten rid of that burden, the burden of having to prove to others that you are someone you are not. The burden of your fear.

OM KALI MAHAKALI
OM KALI MAHAKALI
OM KALI MAHAKALI

There are no more tears. You have reconnected with your real you. There is only liberation, freedom. You now think differently than when you walked into the temple. You now understand that there is an empty space where that ego used to be and you can fill it with whatever you want. This empty space is the opportunity to start building something new. You have cornered and eliminated a part of your ego and the fear it used to hold you back. There is still a long way to go, but it is a little bit shorter.

OM KALI MAHAKALI
OM KALI MAHAKALI
OM KALI MAHAKALI
OM KALI MAHAKALI
OM KALI MAHAKALI
OM KALI MAHAKALI

You give thanks, kneel and prostrate yourself in front of her with your hands on the floor. You feel gratefulness, respect and acknowledgement. You have found a new travel companion who will never leave your side. It is the true friendship of someone who is going to tell you not what you want to hear, but what you need to hear in order to advance.

When you stand up, she speaks to you: "You now carry the treasure of emptiness," she says. "You have the treasure of being nobody; choose carefully what you put in that precious empty space."

You thank her again and again. You feel welcome in this place and you struggle to leave. You were afraid when you walked in – remember? You have overcome that fear and thanks to that you have started to move forward.

You walk out of the temple. You feel light and liberated. You don't care anymore what others think about you. You don't need to. You promise, looking at the image of Kali at the entrance to the temple that looked terrifying when you first entered, that you will treasure that emptiness, you will keep it clean and tidily empty. Only the small things that really matter will decorate that space

You have discovered one of the greatest secrets of self-knowledge and personal development: the destruction of negativity, of implants. You now understand the role of Shiva the destroyer and creator. You understand there is nothing more valuable than an empty space without a single falsehood. You understand that inside you is a gigantic palace filled with light that you have been filling with junk for as long as you can remember. You now know that what is truly valuable is the space, not the things you fill it with. There is still a lot to eliminate, but something important has just changed within you.

Thank you, Kali.

> *OM KALI MAHAKALI*
> *OM KALI MAHAKALI*
> *OM KALI MAHAKALI*

Well done.

Beyond the specific matter you have worked on, this exercise will have been a success if in the future you ask yourself how much of your ego is motivating a decision before following through on it It will have been a success if when you are afraid to do something, you decide to face down that fear and overcome it.

I would like to add something that some might find out of place. It is an analogy between houses and people. Houses can accumulate countless objects, memories of a past life, memories of the lives of other people, furniture and knick-knacks that aren't worth anything to anyone anymore, clothes that have not been worn in a long time and will never be worn again, old papers... It is worth studying the relationship between the state someone is in and the state of his house. I am not talking about luxuries, but about energies. Some houses contain so many things they cannot breathe. Every object, every souvenir, every paper, every clothing item... Every one of them is a story that ties you to the past and drains your energy. I have often witnessed the sense of liberation that comes with cleaning out a house, "emptying" it of useless items, giving them away, selling them to gain a new space. We hesitate over every object: "Should I give it away or keep it? I would be sad to let it go...". It is a wonderful exercise of detachment and liberation. I have observed people change after making this effort I would dare to call a deep exercise. They are completely transformed. Kali will not hesitate to destroy the negativity that is inside you. Let's learn from her by applying it to the spaces we inhabit. Only good things can come from it. We will then be a lot more selective when it comes to bringing things into the house. Like in your inner self, you will only bring constructive things inside. I am not talking about impoverishing your home. What I mean is that if you place an object inside it, be it a painting or a piece of furniture, it should add positive energy and not drain energy. The analogy is intriguing. I recommend you try this exercise of detaching yourself from your objects and freeing up space in your house. It will surprise you.

During this lesson we have tackled one of the most complex aspects of self-knowledge and evolution. We have studied our fears and the ego that brings them about. We have become more aware of the time invested in empty matters. We have worked with Kali, destroyer of fears, and we have learned the concept of inner emptiness, a new space full of opportunities. We might even have changed the way we are going to behave from now on.

LESSON 7

The New Stage: The Temple of Ganesha

At this point in the course, you are in possession of enough self-knowledge and deprogramming tools to seriously consider starting a new stage, if you haven't already, maybe even without realizing.

New stages are the fruit of earlier stages. The new stage would not be possible without our past experiences. Our mistakes, lessons learned, even those we once thought were good for nothing, are the pillars of our being. Good people, toxic people, health, disease, joy, sadness... It has all been necessary to reach this point. We will continue to live good and bad situations and we will have the capacity to manage them and take them for what they are worth. That is why we must be thankful for all the things we have been through, both the good and the bad. It has all been a learning process that will help you make decisions in the future.

"New stage" is a flexible concept. It could be a new inner stage, it could be one more chapter in the stage you are currently living, it could be a complete break from everything... The new stage is a stage in which our conscience is renewed day by day. No matter how much we take care of ourselves energetically, small contaminants will continue to adhere to us, like junk programs that are installed on our computer without us realizing. But now we have Shiva the destroyer and creator ready to help whenever we need him.

The new stage is the empty space we discovered in the temple of Kali. A holy place only you are going to manage.

The new stage is a stage free from addictions that aim to benumb your soul – you have learned to work on that with Hanuman.

The new stage is a stage in which you will reconnect with your gifts, the treasures of a soul whose wisdom is boundless, like the gift library you found in the temple of Saraswati.

LESSON 7 – THE NEW STAGE

The new stage is a stage during which we will keep our physical body under control, eliminating negativities just like Krishna taught us to do in his temple.

The sum of these stages is a series of solid pillars on which we will build our new daily life. Every decision we make, no matter how small or insignificant it may seem, can be a symptom or a catalyst of a new stage. By "new stage" I do not necessarily mean a drastic change in our way of being or living. It could also mean acquiring a new habit, a small acceptance or new belief. It could even be the decision to put the past behind us and focus on the present.

I am sure you have already lived several new stages and these experiences, no matter what their polarity, have led you to this moment. These are all lessons learned that have become a part of who you are, sometimes in an orderly fashion, sometimes chaotically, but nevertheless there. If you focus on the great task of scrutinizing, arranging and extracting positive lessons from your life stages, you will realize it is no coincidence that you are going on this journey with me. Often (very often), the experiences we live can lead us to almost traumatic crises. During these moments, we feel like we have made mistakes, lost time, moved backwards... But I honestly do not believe this is the case. Everything you have been through has brought you to this moment.

The lower beings hate change, but once you have them under control and emptied them of fear and ego, they can be your closest allies standing in solid and harmonious positions with your soul. You must always keep them under control because their simple intelligence (which has nothing to do with your higher intelligence) can be easily influenced by new experiences and messages from the outside world. Controlling our lower beings does not make us immune to the social and media noise that surrounds us, unless we were to abandon society altogether and live like hermits. Speaking of hermits, it's interesting how these people renounced everything in order to find their true selves. The search for inner peace is as old as humanity and the ways of finding it have always involved self-knowledge. Hermits, sadhus, cloistered monks... Seclusion and control over one's bodily desires are two points in common between many philosophies for practicing introspection. The point of this course is not for you to become one of them! But you should learn from them. The strength these people need to make such a radical change in their lives is truly admirable. During this course I aim to show you paths to self-knowledge that are compatible with active participation in the world.

Every time I talk about ascetism I remember the great rift that took place about two thousand years ago between the two main sects of Jainism: the Digambaras and the

LESSON 7 – THE NEW STAGE

Svetambaras. Their interpretations of Mahavira's texts were, and continue to be, very different. Renunciation lay at the heart of the schism. The main point of contention was nudity. Digambaras are also known as "those who dress in air" as they even renounced clothing, whereas Svetambaras are known as "those who dress in white" due to the color of their clothes. What strength of will must be necessary to begin a new stage in which complete renunciation takes centerstage. Truly admirable. I recommend Agustín Paniker's book on Jainism if you want to learn more about one of mankind's oldest living philosophies.

Your feelings when thinking about a new beginning might be confusing right now. You know you are taking your first steps, but you still might want clearer signs or more precise instructions on how to move forward. The eternal search for clear signs and precise instructions can be another block in which your lower beings take control and stop you from moving forward if you don't know in which direction to move. New stages are made up of many little decisions you make on a day-to-day basis. I am sure some of these daily decisions will already be influenced by what you have learned so far. The new stage is here from the moment a decision is influenced by this philosophy.

The philosophy of the new stage is a philosophy of adventure and of control over fear and attachments. We will never be completely free from fear and attachments, but we can say that we know how to control them the moment we stop seeing them as stumbling blocks. It would be wrong to talk about the new stage in singular. It would be more precise to talk about "new stages". Every new thought, every step forward, every new discovery is a new stage. Of course, personal projects, professional projects and business projects are all new stages born from our past stages. It is quite common, once you have entered the world of self-knowledge, for your work life to evolve as a result. Parameters change and new opportunities present themselves. I'm not talking about quitting your job, but about slowly discovering a different approach. Jobs, businesses, bear the imprint of the people who work for them. This imprint is a company's legacy. Of course, new job opportunities might also arise. When we gain new knowledge and self-knowledge, it often takes the shape of new projects, often very innovative ones.

During this lesson, I aim to organise the new sensations you must be feeling as a result of all the previous lessons, to put them into focus and transform them into more changes. I don't want to turn your life upside down! Or maybe I do; that depends entirely on you and your personal circumstances. These can sometimes be complicated and external changes cannot be put

LESSON 7 – THE NEW STAGE

into practice, but there is no excuse not to put internal changes into practice.

There is no doubt Kali did or is doing a good job creating that empty space inside you, the famous "nothing". That emptiness, that clean slate, is as beneficial as cleaning your house and throwing out all your old, broken and obsolete belongings. The house is then empty and looks much larger. You will think twice before filling it again with items that will drain your energies.

This concept, this image, is key for ordering the storm of inner sensations you are now experiencing. An empty space ready to be decorated only with things that add value. It is up to you who or what you let into this space. You are going to paint the walls any color you like and you are going to carefully arrange your individual experiences in such a way that they are harmonious and have a joint meaning. Each item is a building block of the new stage; the overall décor must harmonize the energies of all these items in order to bring about the great new stage.

Kali is one of the energies of the great Shiva, the main ascetic, destroyer and creator. I am sure you have often seen the image of Shiva dancing in the middle of a circle of fire and stamping on the demon of ignorance. It symbolizes new beginnings, destroying everything in order to rebuild following new parameters. The demon of

LESSON 7 – THE NEW STAGE

ignorance can easily be compared to whatever is stopping you from advancing. Your lower beings, ignorant of your Higher Being's potential and capacity to connect with the universal, fall under the sway of false, superficial stimuli. These stimuli penetrate them and if the Higher Being is going through a moment of weakness, this ignorance of reality can spread to it too. I would like you to imagine your inner Shiva and dance on the demon of manipulation and ignorance until you destroy it. This entire course can be summed up in that one image. You are Shiva, Shiva is in you. Dance and destroy the demon of disease, dance and destroy the demon of low self-esteem, of addictions, of fear; and create a new space, a new stage. The great warrior Shiva must impose his new order on your lower beings. He is doing it now and will continue to do so.

We can begin by designing a decoration project for that space on a piece of paper. In this first sketch you are going to express yourself freely, without giving any consideration to the cost of the project, what it is you want to be, who you want to be. This is a personal and private sketch that does not require anyone's approval. Only your own. Before you start drawing, you must have interiorized all the things we learned in the previous lessons, especially the parts having to do with ego. If an item enters that precious empty space only because it "looks good" or "it will make the space more comfortable for of others so they can keep their lives in order. It is your turn to pick up a spade and start to get rid of all these runes. It will surprise you how much space you will have after you are done. It is up to you what you do with the space once it is clean. There will be only emptiness with its infinite possibilities. Your life project, the space of your new stage.

Like in our previous lessons, write down the first goal of the new stage you want to work on. Keep in mind its elasticity, as it is likely to change. Also, keep the bottle of water nearby.

LET'S MEDITATE

The experience in the temple of Kali has made you understand that many ideas have been implanted in you. There are still lots of implants to discover; it is an intense job that you will carry out over time through perseverance. The precious experience in the temple of Saraswati gave you clues about the nature of your gifts and missions. Applying them to this new stage is in your hands.

You walk aimlessly down the street. You feel light and liberated, filled with the peace that comes with an unmovable desire to make a change. Life on the streets goes on. So many people, so many lights, so many colors and smells. You walk through the throng but somehow feel detached. Everything feels blurry. The void you created

LESSON 7 – THE NEW STAGE

with the help of Kali makes you feel strange. You are not used to carrying this emptiness inside you. You think about the human need to hide and compensate for our shortcomings. The need to go on emptying that empty space clashes with the need to fill it with new values and goals. As you walk, you ask yourself what you want to achieve, where you would like to head towards. You fantasize, you imagine yourself in a variety of situations. You look deep inside yourself for what makes you feel at peace, what makes you feel fulfilled. You discard all desires motivated by ego (Kali is watching) and you start to form an idea of who you want to be and what you want to do. You smile because you have just sketched what you want to do with that beautiful empty space inside you. There are no limits or structures, and you are free to design your future. You walk and you walk, and you now know where to begin. You put your hand in your pocket and find a piece of paper. On it is written the goal you have in mind, your first goal during this new stage you are entering after the intense work carried out in the previous temples. It is exactly where you want to begin. You go over it in your mind, think about it, think about the impact it will have on yourself, on others, without ego and without fear. No one is going to full your wonderfully empty space with their old furniture anymore, that much is clear.

LESSON 7 – THE NEW STAGE

Lost in thought, you have covered an enormous distance. You have walked so far you have left the city behind. You are in the countryside, surprised at not having noticed how far you have walked. To the right of the main path is a wooden sign in the shape of an arrow with nothing written on it. Naturally, you follow it. The path leads to a wooden cabin. By the door of the cabin you see Ganesha, god of new beginnings, who protects you from and eliminates the obstacles that stop you from entering new stages. You walk up the three steps to enter the cabin and Ganesha, watchful and vigilant, asks you what you have come to do. Surprised, all you can think of is to hand him the piece of paper on which you have written down your project. He reads it carefully, looks at you, writes it down in a book using his own tusk as a quill. He looks at you again and seems to smile. He hands back the piece of paper and the doors open while he says: "Welcome to my temple, your temple, the temple for reaching your goals, the temple for achieving the right vision. Don't be afraid." He says this last word with the palm of his hand facing forwards and you instantly feel protected. Nothing scares you anymore. You smile back and walk in.

The place is quite austere, though much larger that it looked from the outside. On the walls are paintings depicting the life of Ganesha. You choose a place in front of one of them. You like the image of Ganesha running around his parents, Shiva and Parvati. You feel you are in the right place to begin your project. Ganesha has just told you as much: "The temple for reaching your goals." You pull out the piece of paper and realize there is an extra line on it that wasn't there before. Ganesha has written on it: "And may it bring you inner peace."

Now you feel at peace. Some parts of your lower beings are still trying to dig up past memories to rob you of this sense of peace, but thanks to the wonderful emptiness you have inside, they cannot find anything to disturb you with. In your mind, the requests you are going to make in this temple to eliminate obstacles are clear. You visualize them and carefully introduce that goal into your inner self. You imagine it like a box, austere like the temple you are sitting in, but rich on the inside, filled with much of you and your new being. You imagine yourself lovingly picking up that box and putting it in that perfectly empty and harmonious space inside you. It's interesting to see how a box so small can add such a rich sense of wellbeing to your inner palace. You don't want to lose that harmony for anything in the world. Sitting in front of the box, you feel you must make some modifications to your request. You unfold the paper, pick up the pencil and write down in your own words what Ganesha has told you. You read the goal once again and adjust it so that your request will not only bring you inner peace but also spread it to others.

You know it is not easy and that you will face both internal and external obstacles. You ask Ganesha to help you overcome them.

> *OM GAM GANAPATAYE NAMAHA*
> *OM GAM GANAPATAYE NAMAHA*
> *OM GAM GANAPATAYE NAMAHA*

This mantra has emerged from deep inside you, even though you had never heard it before. You understand that it is the expression of your energetic language, your soul's request for Ganesha to help you with this process. You feel that it is a very powerful mantra, it is a petition for help facing the inner and outer obstacles that will try to make your project fail, and it is a summons for Ganesha and his power.

> *OM GAM GANAPATAYE NAMAHA*
> *OM GAM GANAPATAYE NAMAHA*
> *OM GAM GANAPATAYE NAMAHA*

You feel excited because you know that Ganesha is going to be inside you to help. You feel him near you, kind and caring, but also strong and determined.

While still holding the paper and pencil, you remember what he told you at the entrance to the temple: "The right vision." Now you understand its deeper meaning. To control your inner emotions in order to make the right choices. These right choices, born from a correct vision, will help you overcome the obstacles and reach your goals. The correct vision is being in harmony with your soul. You understand that this concept is key, and you write it down on your piece of paper and underline it.

> *OM GAM GANAPATAYE NAMAHA*
> *OM GAM GANAPATAYE NAMAHA*
> *OM GAM GANAPATAYE NAMAHA*

The vibrations of the mantra make your inner water vibrate as it is charged with the energy of your will. You drink light-water that instantly transforms inside you. This water now also contains your new life project.

You put the piece of paper and pencil in the box, close it and place it lovingly in your inner empty space.

You look at the image of Ganesha on the wall and smile, not understanding it. You again hear someone speak slowly behind you:

Ganesha and his athletic brother Kartikeya had a goal that would make them happier: to find a wife. Their parents, Shiva and Parvati, told them that the first one to travel around the world and come back would marry first. Ganesha was not as fit as his brother but he still beat him. His fitness was not an obstacle; he overcame it. It took Kartikeya many years to travel around the world and back. Ganesha, as shown in the painting, ran seven times around his parents. This surprised them and they asked for explanations. He argued that they are the Divine Mother and Father, the entire earth, the entire universe, and he therefore considered he had won the race. His parents agreed.

These words strengthen your conviction that with the right vision, you will always find a way to reach your goals. You look at the image and smile. You know that Ganesha is also going to be your ally and will help you find this correct vision, the right decisions that will lead you to your noble goals. The new decisions you make from now on will be impregnated with the correct vision.

OM GAM GANAPATAYE NAMAHA
OM GAM GANAPATAYE NAMAHA
OM GAM GANAPATAYE NAMAHA
OM GAM GANAPATAYE NAMAHA
OM GAM GANAPATAYE NAMAHA
OM GAM GANAPATAYE NAMAHA

Your eyes, like so many times before, well up with tears and as they slowly disappear you see your innermost self as a splendid void containing only a box that is now bright and golden. Its light, the light of your next project, lights up the entire space. You look at it and it is spotless, perfect, an ideal space with only one project, only this project is not a one-off, it is for life.

LESSON 7 – THE NEW STAGE

There is a solid door safeguarding your inner self. You lift your hand to your neck and remember the key you found in the fountain near the temple of Krishna. You knew it was for you and so it is. It is the sacred key that locks out negativity and all things that stop your dreams from coming true. You walk towards the door, try the key and, as you suspected, it opens. You look proudly at your innermost space and leave the room, locking the door carefully behind you, and now you are outdoors – back in the city, oddly enough, in the midst of its joy and anarchy, with its good things and not so good things, its people, its problems, its happiness. You look back at the door and it is gone. It will only appear when you really need to open it. Only you have power over it.

You begin the journey back. You go home, you return changed, stronger and determined. You feel peace, you feel like you could reach the end of the universe and overcome every obstacle in the way. You go home feeling like a new and liberated person. You go home knowing yourself wiser.

You look at your house, your things, you go out for a walk, to work... Nothing much has changed during all this time, but you see things in a different light. You now see the reasons why you are here – your circumstances, your life – from a different perspective. Everything is now much simpler, even the difficult parts. You have come back home but you are a different person. Perhaps no one will notice. You don't care. You have nothing to prove. The correct vision is the one that will influence your dozens of daily decisions. Criticisms and attempts at manipulation are not going to find a way into you. A key hangs around your neck and only your soul can make the door appear.

Well done.

During this lesson we have brought together all the things we have learned in order to build a new space inside our innermost selves. We have become aware of the holiness of that space and of the importance of everything that is going to enter into your life from this moment on. Ganesha has helped us clean the paths to this new stage.

Epilogue

Every person is a world and its circumstances. Everyone has reached this moment by following a different path. No two people can exist in the same point at the same time. This is the wonder of individuality. Nobody is like you and nobody knows better than you where you currently stand. Your point can be stable or complicated, but it is the reality you are currently living. Throughout our physical lives, we are always at an ever-changing point that is often the result of the previous points. A decision made in this precise instant is already a past decision that will affect your future. This course is now over. Everything you have read and experienced is now in the past. Any action, no matter how small, that is a consequence of what I have tried to convey can lead to a chain reaction of subsequent actions. This chain of actions will sometimes branch out and lead to changes not only in yourself but also in those around you.

And now what? Now I recommend you go on with your life but living it in harmony with your soul. Every day we make hundreds of decisions. Every decision will influence you and your surroundings. Many decisions are automatic, even reflexes. I will consider this course a success if from now on, when you have to make a decision, you imagine yourself in one of the inner temples and act in accordance with the lessons we have learned. The chain of events can extend endlessly. Nothing brings me more joy than to imagine you might do even a single thing differently than you would have before reading this book. Just one. I am sure that more actions will follow in its wake.

Well done. Congratulations.

Printed in Great Britain
by Amazon